101 Goalkeeper Training Practices

Andy Elleray

Oakamoor Publishing

Published by Oakamoor Publishing, an imprint of Bennion Kearny Limited
6 Woodside
Churnet View Road
Oakamoor
Staffordshire
ST10 3AE

www.BennionKearny.com

Cover images: 103tnn/stock.adobe.com; kurkalukas/stock.adobe.com

About the Author

Andy Elleray has been working in the goalkeeping world since the age of 14 and playing in goal since the age of seven. Over the years, his goalkeeping passion has seen him represent England's Blind Football team playing as the sighted goalkeeper as well as working at such clubs as Liverpool and Chelsea in a goalkeeping capacity. He has studied coaching and performance analysis for many years and has a Master's degree in Sports Coaching along with high level FA and UEFA qualifications.

Andy released his first book – *Scientific Approaches to Goalkeeping in Football* – in March 2013 and it aimed to invoke innovative thinking behind the position and investigate areas such as psychology, biomechanics, performance analysis and practice strictures amongst others. With selected exercises taken from his first book, *65 Goalkeeper Training Exercises* was published in 2017 and promotes different games within a goalkeeping environment in a quick and easy format. In 2018, Andy releases his follow-up: *50 More Goalkeeper Training Exercises*.

Over the past five years, Andy has been working in Women's football as Head of Goalkeeping Development at Birmingham City Ladies alongside the women's international age group teams and the regional excellence pathway – while also holding a position as academy goalkeeping coach at the boy's side of the club.

Table of Contents

Introduction

This third volume of goalkeeping training exercises focuses on two extremes on the goalkeeper-coaching spectrum: working with one goalkeeper, and then the goalkeepers working with the team (where the main emphasis is on outcomes). Although at times, the goalkeeper in the team environment isn't thought about enough (or planned for) by coaches, the suggestions here will directly translate into team-based objectives as well.

The first section of the book will showcase training exercises designed for just one goalkeeper working with one coach. Like previous books, the exercises will look to develop different skills and attributes that the goalkeeper needs to be proficient in, during a match. For clubs or environments without a dedicated goalkeeping coach, these practices will be valuable to give your goalkeeper the extra bit of training they require to enhance their performance. Also, for parents who have a child that plays (or is aspiring to play) in goal, these exercises can help set the scene and provide skills work that will allow them to improve in a variety of different areas.

The idea is to look to recreate and replicate game situations – this might include movements around the goalmouth, recovery saves, and less prescribed handling practices involving high amounts of decision making. Of course, with one goalkeeper, the amount of repetitive practice will be high which will give the goalkeeper plenty of opportunities to work on certain areas of their performance. In the diagrams, equipment such as mannequins can be replaced with poles or cones if not available – mannequins are used to act as bodies, vision blockers, and for deflections.

In the learning detail section, the tactical and social/environmental elements will be taken out for most of the practices. Not because they're not important but because most of the messages are the same. These would include building in distribution after handling elements where appropriate, being in realistic match positions, for the goalkeeper's work to operate at the appropriate intensity (novice vs. elite), and for the coaching environment to be pitched at where the goalkeeper needs it to be, based upon their stage of development.

The second section will go through a series of practices designed for a group of goalkeepers to work on a variety of different attributes – some of these range from basic warm-ups to more complex match situations.

The third section of the book will provide some ideas and examples on how to integrate goalkeepers into the team-based environment, and how to make them a focus within parts of the session specifically. They will look to highlight some tactical empathy as well as the general technical and physical skills that will be tested; examples will include dealing with pressure, communication/information/organisation, and when to defend the goal or space.

As with previous books, all the exercises can be adapted to any specific environment and tailored to how the reader sees fit. Again, the message is to *set the scene*, so the goalkeeper can express themselves and develop the necessary tools required to achieve their potential. The exercises are not necessarily about telling players 'how' to be goalkeepers, as every player will approach the position differently, as well (of course) as each club.

Diving Mechanics

When talking about a goalkeeper's diving mechanics, the focus is on *how* and *when* a player performs these actions. Is their action appropriate to the height, pace, and trajectory of the ball? The timing of these actions is crucial to give the GK the greatest opportunity to protect the goal.

Some examples would be a one-step dive where the GK moves from their set position using one-step towards the ball, a multiple step dive where the ball will be out of the GK's initial reach (so they will have to shift their feet towards the ball in order to cover more ground), and a negative dive step which is where the GK removes the step towards the ball and lowers their head and hands to attempt to reach the ball.

Diving fluency is related to dive mechanics and is something that takes time to develop; it incorporates strength, power, and general coordination. Can the GK generate power to cover areas of the goal from a standing start when there is no time (due to pace on the ball or a close in position) to move their feet before a dive? When a GK is performing a diving action, be mindful of their centre of mass and if this is going directly towards the ball – across low, medium and high dives. The key is getting momentum *through the ball* to increase dive coverage.

Hand shapes and when to use the different types

Appropriate hand shapes allow keepers to deal with the ball most effectively. The type of ball will affect how a keeper approaches a save with their hands; for example, if the GK is going to deflect or manoeuvre away a fast-paced ball, they don't necessarily need to generate more force on the ball. They just use the existing pace and 'guide' the ball away from the goal. The opposite would be the case, however, if the ball is more 'flighted'; in this situation, the GK needs to generate force to get the ball away from danger – they may move their hands towards the ball to act as a strong barrier, or use a closed fist to punch the ball away.

Where is the best possible place for the GK to manoeuvre the ball if they can't secure or catch it? The usual place is wide of the goal and away from immediate danger – then rebounds aren't an immediate threat. However, other issues impact upon parry or deflection points – what's the pace on the ball? Where is the attempt coming from? Are there any other opposition players in the direct vicinity of the situation? Where are the GK's defenders? The GK won't necessarily be able to assess all of these factors at one time but from a coaching recall and analysis point, greater awareness can be identified (video analysis is great for these situations to break the picture down) and trained.

Does the GK use their top or bottom hand when making a save? The line of thought is that the top hand should stay in the air longer when attempting to save high balls above the head. As a coach, analyse whether the GK has made the correct choice when attempting a save.

Body position (head and hips/footwork)

The correlation between the right head position and making saves is very important – with an incorrect head position, the GK often finds themselves with the wrong body position. A rule of thumb that I use often says that no matter what save is being made – get the head as close to the ball as physically possible. The head will usually dictate body position and overall balance.

When the GK is travelling, do they need to cross their legs to increase their stride pattern or not? The side step is usually used when moving a short distance (but feet must stay close to the ground as the GK may need to stop quickly). The danger in using the wrong step method is that if the cross-over is used and the ball is struck towards the GK, they're not in a position to set themselves and generate movement (due to their legs being crossed over). Vice-versa, if the GK needs to cover a longer distance and they choose to side step, more often than not this is slower. Footwork patterns are also affected by the GK's height, coordination, balance, and ability to generate velocity.

If a GK is moving over a shorter distance, the hands need to be in a higher position as, more often than not, they will be in direct threat of an attempt on goal (e.g., hands need to be ready, nearer a 'set' position shape). If they're travelling over a longer distance, then the ball may not be in direct of them, and they will need to generate momentum to move using their arms. The main point with travelling is that a keeper needs to learn to *decelerate* at the right time (based on the flight/direction of the ball) *and* with their hands in the appropriate position to make a save or engage a cross, etc.

How GKs should communicate with defenders

Communication is an interpersonal skill that has a massive impact on any given situation in football. Aside from simple instructions ("fall back", "man on", etc.) – it can positively and adversely affect the feeling and thoughts of the team. Goalkeeping communication can basically be broken down into two facets:

1. How you say something (the exchange).

2. What you actually say (information).

Verbal communication (oral feedback, instructions, praise) and visual communication (a positive or negative gesture, for example) dominate the goalkeeper's approach. They can also be combined with actions that highlight demeanour and which have impact – such as a player walking away when being spoken to, or not showing some kind of acknowledgement to show they've heard or seen a command.

Body language is often highlighted as an important element to develop in keepers. How you carry yourself on and off the pitch can give off positive or negative vibes. For example, if a GK is showing negative body language before corners or free kicks and shrinks into their shell or displays outward emotion (such as edginess), this can communicate to the opposition that the GK is apprehensive which they can look to exploit.

Frequently, at youth level, I get asked, "How can I get my goalkeeper to talk more?" Well, there's no easy answer, although I would say that two things should be at the forefront of any coach's thinking.

1. Most young keepers don't know what to say

2. And they don't have the confidence to address their team

The first point can relate to tactical understanding. When you're a young goalkeeper, there's so much information to take in, mainly on the technical side (focusing on how to physically save the ball and the situations being faced). In turn, there comes a time when the ball is in close proximity and the GK must focus on their primary role which is to keep the ball out of the net and not worry about communicating verbally or visually. Tactical understanding, and the actions derived from that understanding, comes with experience and recognising game cues takes time to develop. With young GKs, though, I would encourage them to start calling out instructions when they recognise the main dangers and threats that the opposition pose. This might be as simple as telling a player to mark an opposition striker, or to force a player wide away from the goal.

It goes without saying that the goalkeeper can see the whole picture from their position – working on communication can keep their team in solid shape and players in correct positions. That means the keeper should have less work to do in a match.

All commands should be clear, short and sharp, using the appropriate tone of voice. Players *should not* commentate, they are not John Motson! In turn, if they're monotone, and constantly talking, their team will switch off and not respond quickly when actually required. GKs should focus on the players they can directly affect – as when defensive shapes need to be organised when the ball is in the attacking third.

As the coach, it's important to show examples of when to use the directional terms you want your players to learn, either in training, through video recall, or by watching live games a player is not involved in. This is why specific game-based exercises and sessions are so important – along with integration into the team. The book *Let's Talk Soccer* by Gerard Jones is a great introduction to the value and implementation of game calls across a team.

The second point (players don't have the confidence to address their team) is very relevant to the confidence section. Again, it is important for the goalkeeper to integrate with the team to form relationships and create cohesion. I think that if you get the first point right, then the second will take care of itself. The thought of saying the wrong thing or 'not knowing your team' can make you very placid – I speak from experience here!

Of course, when looking to receive the ball, the goalkeeper's commands should be verbal and visual. For example, when wanting to receive the ball on their right foot from a defender, a keeper might say, "Right foot, John" [showing their right hand at the same time]. Making eye contact with the player is also important – especially when leaving the goalmouth to receive a ball. By employing eye contact, the defender can see you change position and not play the ball to where they saw you last – but where you actually are.

Whether verbal or visual, it's crucial in your sessions that a keeper practices both types of communication and that the goalkeeper understands *where* and *when* to use them. The key is to be loud and specific; every goalkeeper is different and personalities will dictate the specifics of communication – but your job, as coach, is to give players the necessary tools and feedback to help them find the approach that works best for them.

The key is to say 'WHAT' to do rather than 'WHAT NOT' to do. Example – say STOP or BLOCK instead of 'no shot'. Players respond to the POSITIVE not the NEGATIVE. Some examples that can be used are as follows:

• "BLOCK" – CENTRAL AREAS – block shots, through balls, and goal scoring opportunities.

• "LOCK" – WIDE AREAS – players lock on, or mark, to deny space and stop the opposition.

• "PRESS" – press the ball as a unit/team, not as an individual, in order to stay compact and in shape.

• "STOP" – deny the opposition time or space.

• "PRESSURE" – pressure on the ball at any given time (in line with the team's tactics).

• "TIME" – player has time on the ball.

• "AWAY" – player(s) needs to deal with the ball – clear or keep possession.

• "KEEPER" – Keeper is coming for the ball.

• "SLIDE" – followed by a direction and/or how far.

• "STEP" – team steps up the pitch (use guidelines on the pitch to assist distances).

• "MARK" – mark players from set pieces and throw-ins.

• "HOLD" – at a particular area on the pitch or defensive line at any point.

• "AFFECT" – remind the team to affect the team in a positive way – e.g., 1v1 defending or being in the correct position.

In a nutshell, all communication should be:

1. CLEAR
2. CONCISE
3. CONTROLLED
4. SPECIFIC
5. APPROPRIATE

Okay, now that we have covered some of the background to this book, it is time to get our hands dirty!

Warm-ups

The purpose of a goalkeeping warm-up is to prepare the goalkeeper for the upcoming training session both physically and psychologically. There are, of course, a whole host of ways to warm-up including pre-activation, stretching, low-level plyometrics, and various movement-based exercises. Over the years, I have used activation and warm-ups to build, develop, and maintain goalkeeper's agility, flexibility, and core strength.

A key component of a goalkeeping warm-up should be to introduce decision-making situations from the very start; and to couple them with physical actions/movements. Also, coaches should base the warm-up and first practices around the main session topic – to introduce similar movement patterns and to build a picture of what to expect (psychologically) for the session.

From a social point of view, warm-ups are very important. This time is often used by goalkeepers to create their own space to prepare for the session mentally. I've been in situations where I've let goalkeepers lead the warm-up when in a small group of three or four – to build up responsibility and ownership, as well as communication skills and confidence. With younger goalkeepers, warm-ups can be used as ice-breakers or to introduce a new topic.

Many of the exercises in the book can be used as warm-ups or lead-ins to the main session – these are stated in the content of each practice. Exercises touch upon mainly the physical and psychological aspects of keeping – as many of the technical aspects of the position stem from a physical perspective. Tactically, of course, goalkeepers will be preparing their distribution, their alertness, and general decision making so that when they begin team-based practices, they are fully able to carry out what's required of them from a tactical point of view.

Within the warm-up phase, the coach can observer a goalkeeper's general movement patterns but also their specific physical capabilities towards a certain element of goalkeeping. For example, what are their jumping mechanics like, since this directly impacts their ability to take crosses. Warm-ups can help form the basis of an individual development plan; in recent years, I have used lots of movement warm-up exercises that aren't necessarily goalkeeping-specific but which help build the fundamental patterns keepers need to perform. They include tasks such as jumping, diving, kicking, and sprinting. For example, I worked with a goalkeeper who, at 14-years of age, was 6ft 1 tall, and struggled a great deal with her movement. Lots of the warm-ups covered in this book enabled her to build her physicality. She is now playing for England and in the top league of women's football in England.

Psychosocially, the coach can observe leadership qualities, group cohesion, and how easily different goalkeepers pick up new skills. On top of this, coaches can analyse a player's ability to make decisions – such as assessing the ball's flight path, and where to position themselves for different distribution methods.

In terms of timings, a thorough and appropriate warm-up is paramount before a session, so don't be afraid to work longer on basic movements and skills before moving on. The older a goalkeeper is, the longer they'll need to warm-up. Bear in mind, as well, that goalkeepers' bodies should not be stressed too much, too soon, if you want them to produce their optimum power and flexibility in the full training session; starting out too intensely can cause injuries. Many coaches send goalkeepers out to a training session before the outfield players to physically prepare as the position can take its toll on the body. At international level, it's common practice for the goalkeepers to have their own specific activation and warm-up procedures before starting any group session.

Individual Goalkeeper Practices

The first section's aims, as stated in the introduction, are based around one goalkeeper working with either a coach, parent, or possibly another goalkeeper.

They are great for environments that may not necessarily be blessed with having a designated goalkeeping coach. The practices allow a team's goalkeeper to receive crucial practice on the foundations of the position.

The practices look to set the scene with learning detail that seeks to give the personnel involved a clear picture of the aims and objectives within each exercise. Each one can be tailored to fit the working GK – in terms of age, agility, and performance requirements.

In some practices, there are multiple diagrams to show, in detail, how they work – but use them as a starting point for further progressions or setup changes that will benefit goalkeepers in all areas of their game.

1

Goalkeeping Themes: Warm-up – general mobility and basic handling.

Practice Objectives: To give the GK a number of repetitions of different movements, footwork, and handling opportunities.

Description: The ball starts with the server who is on ball 1. The GK moves around the mannequin and receives a handling opportunity (volley, clip, scoop save, etc.). They roll the ball back to the server and go behind the mannequin to either ball 2 or 3. Here, the GK can pass the ball into a target (if you have mini goals), dive onto the ball, or move around the ball, for example. They will move to the ball they haven't been to, next, before going back around the mannequin for another handling opportunity. The service can be really varied here and incorporate dives, jumping, or loose balls.

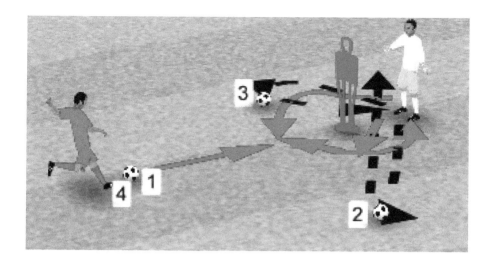

Progressions:

Change the actions the GK is performing.

Alter the angles and distances of the service to change the demands upon the GK.

Learning Detail:

Technical: Consistency and detail of handling and footwork | Efficiency of footwork patterns

Psychological: Concentration with all the four actions (all at a high standard) | Decisions as to the handling techniques to use and where/when to set themselves

Physical: If travelling a short distance, keep hands closer to the body | Focus on balanced and co-ordinated movement, with the upper body still | Ability to decelerate, to be in a set position

2

Goalkeeping Themes: Warm-up – handling and distribution actions.

Practice Objectives: To allow the GK to go through a selection of movements, handling opportunities, and foot contacts.

Description: GK starts behind a mannequin (or pole/cones) and travels in front to receive a strike, in and around their body. They then travel backwards behind the mannequin for a 1-2 pass to the opposite side. The final action is a travel back from action 2 into a dive from the server (any height).

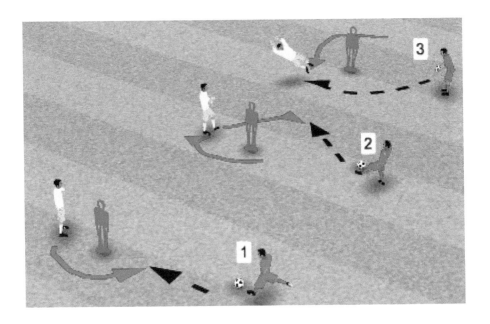

Progressions:

Vary the angles and distances of the service.

Build in other actions – for example, specific movement patterns related to a session's topic.

Learning Detail:

Technical: Consistency and detail of handling and footwork | Efficiency of footwork patterns

Psychological: Concentration relating to all four actions (all at a high standard) | Decision-making for the handling technique to use and where/when to set themselves

Physical: If travelling a short distance, keep hands closer to the body | Focus on balanced and co-ordinated movement with upper body still | Ability to decelerate to be in a set position

3

Goalkeeping Themes: Defending the goal on the angle.

Practice Objectives: To provide the GK with an opportunity to work on their depth in the goal, and their body shape to deal with attempts from an angle.

Description: The ball starts behind the mannequin and is shifted either side for a shot on goal. If the initial contact takes the ball back into the coned box, then the GK should look to perform a recovery save; if the contact takes the ball back into the playing area, the server can have a first time rebound.

Progressions:

Move the start position of the ball laterally and/or take the ball further back.

Give the GK a movement before the strike – for example, travelling across the goal mouth.

Learning Detail:

Technical: Type of hand contact (catch, deflect, or repel) | When and where to use the legs to save the ball | Be able to manoeuvre the ball out of immediate danger from the strike

Tactical: If the touch takes the ball past the line of the mannequin, then the GK should think about engaging the ball

Psychological: Assess the weight and direction of the first touch from the server | Speed of decision on saving response | Bravery to engage the ball if necessary

Physical: Speed and strength and efficiency of limb movement (low, medium, and high) | Balance and control of the set position after the initial touch

4

Goalkeeping Themes: Defending the goal on the angle – with central option.

Practice Objectives: To provide the GK with an opportunity to work on their depth in the goal, and their body shape to deal with attempts from an angle – with progression into a more random practice.

Description: The ball starts behind the mannequin and is shifted either side for a shot on goal. The server can also shift the ball, again, past the second mannequin for a strike at the goal. If the initial contact takes the ball back into the coned box then the GK should look to perform a recovery save; if the contact takes the ball back into the playing area, the server can have a first time rebound.

Progressions:

Move the start position of the ball laterally and/or take the ball further back.

Give the GK a movement before the strike – for example, travelling across the goal mouth.

Learning Detail:

Technical: Type of hand contact (catch, deflect, or repel) | When and where to use the legs to save the ball | Be able to manoeuvre the ball out of immediate danger from the strike

Tactical: If the touch takes the ball past the line of the mannequin, then the GK should think about engaging the ball | Positioning off a second touch across the goal

Psychological: Assess the weight and direction of the first touch from the server |Speed of decision on saving response | Bravery to engage the ball if necessary

Physical: Speed and strength and efficiency of limb movement (low, medium, and high) | Balance and control of the set position after the initial touch

5

Goalkeeping Themes: Travelling across the goal – coverage of different distances.

Practice Objectives: To ensure the GK is comfortable travelling across the goal into attempts where the server is looking to actively score.

Description: The GK steps forwards towards 1, 2 or 3 (coach will call). The GK then travels across the ball to where the server is positioned, to face an attempt on goal.

Progressions:

Change the distance for the GK to travel (as this will change stride/movement patterns).

Move the position of the ball for every repetition so the GK doesn't get into a rhythm; every attempt on goal in a match is different.

Learning Detail:

Technical: Observe the response from the GK and determine whether it is appropriate to the situation | The ability to manoeuvre the ball away from immediate danger | Footwork within the save selection – does the GK have time to shift their feet before a dive or jump, or is it necessary to generate power/momentum from a stationary position

Psychological: Assess where the server is shooting from and decide where to position themselves – looking at depth and angle of the travel across the goal | Being adaptable to the ball's movement and the change of position from the server

Physical: Travel across the goal – stride pattern and ability to decelerate into an appropriate position with body control | Balanced set positions upon control – don't guess or premeditate as the head will dictate the appropriate bodily balance | General agility and co-ordination in diving and jumping actions

6

Goalkeeping Themes: Distribution with angled shot stopping/recovery saves.

Practice Objectives: To give the GK practice on different types of distribution along with exposure to quick changes of the ball before an attempt on goal.

Description: The GK starts with the ball outside the line of the post. They take a touch into the playing area and play the ball into the server (start with a clip or driven pass) and follow their pass. The server then rolls or touches the ball in front of them for a strike on goal (A). If the GK claims the ball, they throw the ball to the server who will move at an angle. When they receive the ball, they have one touch before an attempt on goal (B). If the initial shot goes in, or the GK saves the ball behind/away from the goal, the server will give the GK a second save from ball 1.

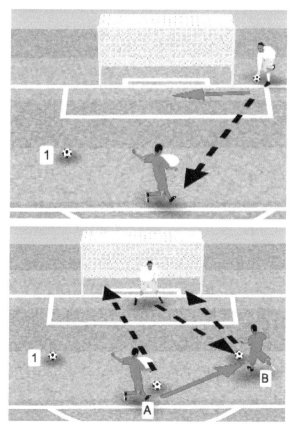

Progressions:

Change the angles and distances where the receiving player is positioned.

Add mannequins or vision blockers to provide different challenges for the GK.

Learning Detail:

Technical: Initial consistency, weight, and direction of the distribution to the server | Attacking the ball forwards with the hands – or feet if appropriate | Efficiency of footwork to gain body momentum to cover the goal from a dive or jumping action

Tactical: Ability to adjust position in the goal depending on the server's first touch | Decision off the GK's first contact on the ball – recovery save or defend the goal

Psychological: Adaptability to assess the changes of movement of the ball, picking up the relevant cues to advance/drop etc. | Save selection decision – appropriateness and the speed with which this is done

Physical: Focus on body control (balance/co-ordination) | Speed to engage the ball if necessary on recovery saves | Arm and lower limb extension | Head as close to the ball as possible on lateral saves (diving, jumping, and leg saves)

7

Goalkeeping Themes: Distribution with central shot stopping.

Practice Objectives: To challenge the GK's speed of thought in making different kinds of saves along with igniting attacks (transitional focus).

Description: The GK starts with the ball outside the line of the post; they play the ball (driven, clip, or drilled pass) to the server. The GK follows their pass into the goal mouth. The server will take a touch and then look to score after this initial contact. If the GK claims the ball, they can distribute into the small mini goal or target area. If the ball is left in the penalty area (or playing area) after the GK's initial contact, they can look to rebounds, giving the GK a recovery save/decision.

Progressions:

Change distribution length to work on counter attacking methods.

Take out, or move, mannequins to provide different vision blockers.

Learning Detail:

Technical: Initial consistency, weight, and direction of the distribution to the server | Technical response to the initial shot on goal | Individual effectiveness to defend the goal

Tactical: Ability to adjust position in the goal depending on the server's first touch | Decision off the GK's first contact on the ball – recovery save or defend the goal | Positioning in relation to the mannequins (defenders)

Psychological: Adaptability to assess the changes of movement of the ball, picking up the relevant cues to advance/drop etc. | Save selection decision – appropriateness and the speed with which this is done

Physical: Focus on body control (balance/co-ordination) | Speed to engage the ball if necessary on recovery saves | Arm and lower limb extension | Head as close to the ball as possible on lateral saves (diving, jumping, and leg saves)

8

Goalkeeping Themes: General handling techniques incorporating 1v1 situations.

Practice Objectives: To allow the GK to gain confidence in 1v1 situations and to practice their timing of engagement/variation of techniques.

Description: The ball starts with the server from a central area. They take a touch and strike at goal (looking to test the keeper but not necessarily score). Once the GK claims the ball, they roll the ball in-between either gate on the side of the 6-yard box (shown as 1 and 2). The server will then advance to the ball and strike the ball first time and try to score.

Progressions:

The GK can throw the ball at different heights to the server to vary their first touch; this will affect their initial movement and/or position.

Change the angle and distances of the receiving server.

Learning Detail:

Technical: Block, smother, or leg save? | Angle of approach to the ball | Close observation of head position in relation to their body but also the ball

Psychological: Decision of when, where, and how to engage the ball – with a focus on the relevant cues (a bigger first touch or the ball being out of the server's feet) | Appropriate technique for responding to the distance the GK finds themselves away from the ball

Physical: Stride pattern when covering the space | Ability of the GK to remain strong and provide a physical barrier | Flexibility and speed of upper and lower limbs to respond to the varying heights and directions of the ball

9

Goalkeeping Themes: Cut backs, reflexes/reactions, and counter attacks.

Practice Objectives: To provide the GK with a scenario where they have to think, and respond quickly, to cutbacks and strikes on the ball where the odds are in the server's favour to score.

Description: The server starts with the ball, with the GK facing them. They punch pass the ball to the rebound board with the ball coming off at different angles. The GK will follow the ball to respond to the new position of the ball. The server will then take a first-time shot on goal. If the GK claims the ball, they can break the line of the mannequins and look to start counter attacks (the goal is shorter just to show an example).

Progressions:

Bring in rebounds from the server if the ball is left in the playing zone – this can expose recovery saves/decisions.

Change the distance and angle of the pass from the server, along with the rebound board position.

Learning Detail:

Technical: Hand position on set position – not too low as the legs can defend balls in and around the body if the ball is struck there | Technical response – not necessarily orthodox techniques from this range – individual effectiveness/style

Tactical: Engage the ball or drop off to defend the goal giving the GK more reaction time | position off the strike – be in the half of the goal where the strike will take place

Psychological: Ability to assess the ball position after the rebound board and the type of contact the server makes from their shot | Don't track the ball all the way off the rebound board – look to where the contact will take place

Physical: Upper and lower limb speed | Ability to generate power from a stationary position | Where, when, and how to set – is there time in this situation?

10

Goalkeeping Themes: Warm-up – focusing on dive techniques.

Practice Objectives: To give the GK some repetition in dive techniques with an emphasis on speed and tempo of actions.

Description: 1 – The server (who occupies all three positions in the diagram) plays a 1-2 pass with the GK. 2 – The server plays the ball either side of the GK for a dive. 3 – GK will return to speed as quickly as possible, roll the ball to the server who will give them a mid-range or a high dive. Distances can vary with longer distances bringing in the potential to focus on footwork before the dive (not just the set position).

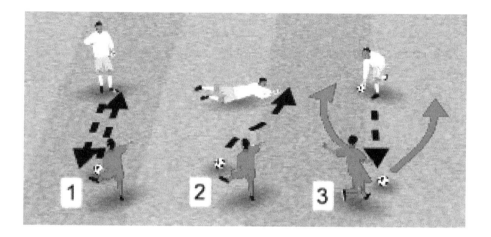

Progressions:

Angle of the server, not just passing from a central position.

Make the actions random (e.g. not prescribed) to increase the psychological challenge.

Learning Detail:

Technical: Hand shape and positioning on dives | Consistency in detail of passing, catching, and throwing | Going through the ball – not stopping at the point of hand impact

Psychological: Response to the ball in terms of its direction, pace, and height in order to execute the dive | Focus on watching the ball into the hands

Physical: Speed and control of the dive (with observation on footwork and leg step | The ability to co-ordinate different movements in quick succession

11

Goalkeeping Themes: Warm-up – focusing on handling, general activation, and footwork.

Practice Objectives: To allow the GK to go through a whole range of handling techniques, movement patterns, and general activation actions – which gradual get more intense.

Description: The ball will start with the server at a random distance away from a 4-yard goal. The GK will face the server and receive a handling opportunity. Once the GK has dealt with the attempt, they will spin off either left or right and complete some dynamic footwork patterns (jumps, quick feet around cones, both lateral and vertical). They will then return to the small goal (jog) and the process will begin again. Work for 1 minute or 6 repetitions.

Progressions:

Change footwork patterns and the distance of the server.

Learning Detail:

Technical: Handling consistency and point of contact | Set position for the server's strike | Head and hand position whilst travelling around the practice

Psychological: Attention to detail with the movements – is the GK balanced and in control of their body?

Physical: Focus on balance and co-ordination within the different movement patterns | Look to increase intensity as this practice progresses

12

Goalkeeping Themes: Reflex work with a focus on saving on the move/reacting to different ball flights and trajectories.

Practice Objectives: To test the GK's ability to produce unorthodox movements in order to keep the ball from going into the goal. There may not always be time to set, so having the capacity to re-adjust one's body is paramount – especially if the ball is travelling/changing position quickly.

Description: The GK starts with the ball in their hands to either side of a pre-determined sized goal (mini 4-yard goals shown). The server is stationed between 4 and 8 yards away from the goal and with every repetition they change slightly. The GK volleys the ball to the server who catches the ball and volleys back as soon as they have control of the ball. The GK must follow their pass towards the goal laterally and attempt to save the ball. Picture 2 is the same setup but with 2 mini goals which will allow the GK to work on reflex saves where they have to move back the way they've come. Set the GK a target number of saves from 10 served balls.

Progressions:

Alter the distance and direction of the server.

Change the distribution method – to bring in different trajectories of service from the server.

Learning Detail:

Technical: How is the ball saved? Hand, leg or body - is this appropriate to the attempted faced? | Promote the fundamentals but encourage creativity and individual effectiveness

Psychological: Not to dwell on goals going in as this practice is designed to challenge the GK | The speed with which the GK assesses the flight, pace, and direction of the ball | Desire to save!

Physical: Having the necessary flexibility and co-ordination to move limbs into 'un-natural' positions | Ability to be 'set' upon the striker's contact with the ball (if possible) | The power to generate force into their own momentum and to manoeuvre the ball away from immediate danger

13

Goalkeeping Themes: Long range shot stopping – variations of start positions and ball movement.

Practice Objectives: To expose the GK to different long-range shot stopping situations where they will have to respond to changing ball movement, potential deflections, and adapt their positioning in a fast but controlled manner.

Description: There are three variations of this practice. 1 – The server starts with the ball, takes a touch, and strikes the ball through the mannequins. 2 – The GK starts with the ball, plays over the top of the mannequin for the server to control, then strikes back at goal first time (this will bring in different strike points from the server, such as a volley or half volley). 3 – The server starts with the ball on the apex of the penalty box, they play the ball into the GK, so they can play back to the server first time. At this point, the GK travels into the goalmouth to take up an appropriate position whilst the server takes a touch towards the mannequins and strikes at goal to score.

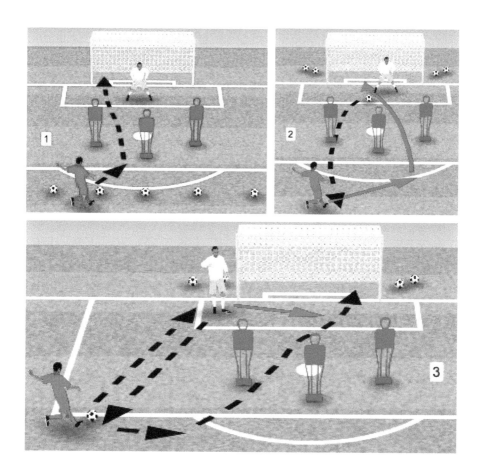

Progressions:

Add in distribution to all three practices if the GK claims the ball – working on 'what next?' after gaining control of the ball.

Look to build in recovery decisions after the initial contact from GK.

Change the position of the mannequins and the various start points in each variation of the practice.

Learning Detail:

Technical: Accuracy and playability of distribution where necessary |Response to the attempt on goal | Look at top vs bottom hand saves

Tactical: Positioning in relation to the ball and/or specific scenario the GK finds themselves in |Positioning off a bouncing or an angled ball – how does this change the GK's goal protecting position?

Psychological: Early assessment of the ball (flight, pace, and trajectory) |Responding quickly to any deflections or contacts off mannequins |Bravery to try new techniques and not being afraid to keep the ball out in 'unorthodox' manners

Physical: Footwork on goal coverage – step patterns, timing of dive/jump, and getting momentum through the ball |Strength and flexibility of body and limbs whilst making saves

14

Goalkeeping Themes: First touch and passing variations.

Practice Objectives: To give the GK practice on receiving the ball away from pressure and playing from outside the line of the posts into target zones/players.

Description: The server starts with the ball. Depending on the age/ability of the GK, find an appropriate distance to start and also an appropriate position for the GK to start. The GK starts in line with the server and supports either left or right of the mannequin. They receive the ball, taking a touch, then play into the target goal (this can a pole, mannequins, etc depending on the focus – for example, if playing into a player, use a mannequin; if working on ball connection using a goal).

Progressions:

Vary distances and angles of support.

Use realistic distances for the passing technique worked on – for example, with a clipped pass with height on, use an obstacle to go over to get the right trajectory.

Learning Detail:

Technical: Observation on the technique used – looking at foot contact on the strike of the ball | Enable the GK to find their optimum first touch angle/weight in order to play effectively off the next touch on the ball

Tactical: Support away from the mannequin to give more time | When working on a specific type of pass, analysis as to whether a receiving player would be able to secure or use that ball (making the ball playable)

Psychological: Consistency and detail of first touch and passing | Attention to the choice of technique, depending on the range of pass the GK is working on

Physical: Ability to move laterally into position but keep an open body shape and stable kicking base | Kicking mechanics and co-ordination – look at non-kicking foot when GK is striking the ball

15

Goalkeeping Themes: 1v1 and close-range save techniques – focus on blocking and leg saves.

Practice Objectives: To provide the environment for the GK to develop their timing, bravery, and assessment of close-range situations where 1v1 techniques are needed.

Description: The distance between the goals and the server can vary depending on age and ability but consider when and where these 1v1 techniques would take place. There are two different ways in which the attempt on goal can be initiated. 1 – The GK and server are playing 1-2 passes with each other. Whenever the server decides, they can move to either ball and look to score first time in the mini goals. 2 – The GK and server are again playing 1-2 passes (or can also be throws, volleys, or any other distribution type) and when the server has the ball under control, they roll it towards the server and try to score off the next touch.

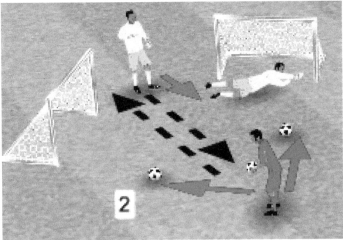

Progressions:

See which practice variation works best for the GK.

If mini goals aren't available, then use poles or cones which can be altered in size depending on the GK's requirements.

Learning Detail:

Technical: Key focus on the GK's head position and ability to be in a position to cover the goal | Flexible lower body – not being too narrow | Technical response in relation to the height of the ball – utilisation and timing of the leg save

Psychological: The GK's desire to put their body on the line to keep the ball out the goal | Speed of technical selection and application | Confidence to try new techniques and movements

Physical: Strength of body and limbs – look to be a barrier and a wall | Speed to cover the distance the goals are away from the GK's starting position

16

Goalkeeping Themes: Saves from 4-8 yards – focussing on reaction and agility.

Practice Objectives: To expose the GK to a picture where they have to respond and move quickly to attempts on goal from a short distance – last ditch efforts and 'big saves' are the order of the day.

Description: The GK starts with the ball in their possession facing a rebound board/net. They roll or pass the ball towards the rebound board and then face the shot from the server. The GK will need to travel across the goalmouth and the server can start anywhere between the mannequin and the post. If mannequins are not available, then poles or other obstacles can be used.

Progressions:

Work both sides of the goal – think about the GK looking towards the point of contact from the player (and not tracking the ball all the way across the goal).

If the ball is left in the playing area, then the server can attempt rebounds. Weigh up the situation as if the GK makes a great save but, in doing so, the ball is left in the area; in this case, hitting the ball back in might not be the best option!

In the diagram, ball 2 can be a second shot on goal.

Learning Detail:

Technical: Footwork across the goal – observe stride pattern in response to the ball and the distance that is needed to be covered | Body part to save – closest part to the ball vs hands?

Tactical: Positioning in response to the moving ball – how far to travel based upon the speed and direction of the ball - can the GK engage the ball?

Psychological: Desire to keep the ball out of the goal! | Recognition that this situation is overloaded in favour of the attacker – what does success look like in terms of the number of saves?

Physical: Head position upon all saves – get this as close to the ball as possible | Speed and bodily control across the goal | Flexibility to perform 'unorthodox' movements and actions

17

Goalkeeping Themes: Saves from 4-8 yards – focussing on reaction and agility.

Practice Objectives: To expose the GK to a picture where they have to respond and move quickly to attempts on goal from a short distance – last ditch efforts and 'big saves' are, once again, the order of the day.

Description: The server starts with the ball behind the central mannequin; they then decide when they touch or turn on the ball and strike first time to try and score. The GK can start where they want in terms of depth – and this should be a key coaching outcome for the GK coach to analyse.

Progressions:

Work left and right sided.

Change the distance of the mannequins away from goal to work on different outcomes.

Learning Detail:

Technical: Initial stance if the GK can't close the space – high hands vs low hands? | How and when to use leg saves – look at the timing of this execution | Strong body – don't let the ball just hit the body – guide, block or manoeuvre the ball away from goal/close in players

Tactical: Positioning in response to the moving ball – how far to travel based upon the speed and direction of the ball - can the GK engage the ball?

Psychological: Desire to keep the ball out of the goal! | Recognition that this situation is overloaded in favour of the attacker – what does success look like in terms of the number of saves?

Physical: Head position upon all saves – get this as close to the ball as possible | Speed and bodily control across the goal | Flexibility to perform 'unorthodox' movements and actions

18

Goalkeeping Themes: Shot stopping work where the GK is out of position.

Practice Objectives: To allow the GK to work on situations where they've been found out of position and how best to defend the goal from this. Such questions as when to set, and how to best position themselves, will be key ones that a coach must consider and pose to the GK.

Description: The ball starts with the server, with the GK in any position they want in the goalmouth (emphasise the practice objective). The GK will have their eyes on the server and when they touch the ball out of their feet the GK can then move and the sever will look to score. The server will start from a different position each time. Have distance zones to begin with; for example, the first set of 10 will be between 10-14 yards – think about the difficulty for the GK based upon who you're working with.

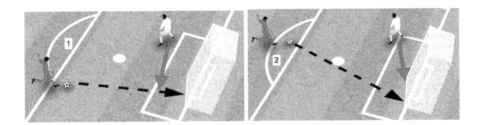

Progressions:

The ball can start loose and not at the attacker's feet – this will give the GK a different decision in terms of positioning and how/where they need to travel around the goalmouth.

Emphasise left and right foot attempts on goal as well as different types of shot on goal (drilled, curled, or placed, for example). Also add mannequins to act as vision blockers and traffic.

Learning Detail:

Technical: General shot stopping principles – focus on the GK's ability to adapt their technical decision based upon the specific picture that is happening

Tactical: When and where to set – look at setting (even if slightly out of position) to give the GK the best chance of moving in all directions |

Think about dropping first rather than travelling laterally which will give more time to respond

Psychological: The difficulty of the practice will determine mainly how quickly the GK can assess the picture in front of them – ball/player position and the best route to defend the goal

Physical: Speed of travel but also the speed of deceleration and set at the right time | Speed of limbs and the ability of the GK to get their head as close to the ball as possible for each action

19

Goalkeeping Themes: General handling techniques with a big emphasis on efficiency of footwork and movement patterns.

Practice Objectives: To test the GK's ability to show fast and balanced footwork to cover a variety of distances and angles.

Description: The ball will start with the server from a pre-determined distance (can stay the same or vary in angle for each repetition). Their objective is to land the ball to bounce in the grid – the GK will have to stop the ball bouncing. The GK can either look to catch the ball, or if they need to deflect or repel the ball away, then their decision needs to be based upon factors such as the pace, flight, trajectory and direction of the ball. The GK's grid can be any size – the larger the grid the bigger the distance the GK will need to cover, hence the greater the difficulty.

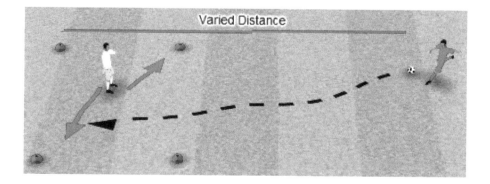

Varied Distance

Progressions:

The server can move each repetition laterally or vertically.

The GK can distribute back to the server if they secure the ball to practise different techniques.

Learning Detail:

Technical: Can the GK catch the ball or do they need to change their hand shape to perform a deflection, parry, or a repel away from the grid? | Can they adapt this technical decision quickly, based upon the ball that's played into the grid?

Psychological: Desire to not give up on any ball that's played in | Early assessment and execution of the movement pattern required to get to the ball as quickly and efficiently as possible

Physical: Speed and size of stride pattern – is this effective based upon the ball that's played towards them? | Ability of the GK to move 360 degrees – if weak in certain directions, target this more with the service

20

Goalkeeping Themes: Close-range shot stopping with a focus on agility, and the ability to generate force from a standing stance.

Practice Objectives: To expose the GK to fast attempts on goal where it's not always possible for them to move their feet to gain momentum for diving and jumping actions.

Description: The ball starts from position 1 in the diagram where the server will shoot on goal from the pole to the mannequin (similar to a penalty). The GK will attempt to save this ball and once they've made an initial contact, the server will then move to ball 2 and shoot in the opposite half of the goal – both attempts to score.

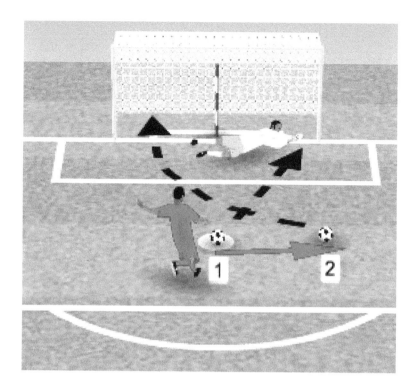

Progressions:

Work both sides of the goal and change the angle and positioning of ball 2.

Learning Detail:

Technical: Strong diving action and speed of handling | Whether the GK goes with one or two hands for these attempts – one hand, at times, can allow for a greater reach

Psychological: Maintain focus and emotional control – keep a clear mind for both attempts | Overall speed to assess and execute the desired actions from the GK – picking up the relevant environmental cues

Physical: Ability to generate velocity from a standing stance to cover as much distance as possible – the faster the shot on goal, the less time to produce footwork | Body shape and stance for getting off the ground and returning to feet is critical – is the GK in a position to step into the dive and generate enough force to cover the opposite half of the goal?

Group Goalkeeper Practices

The second section of this book revolves around group goalkeeper practices. The aim is to provide different types of practice that stretch and challenge those involved, whilst still addressing the basic foundations of goalkeeping.

All of these practices have been used at various levels of football from grassroots right up to elite youth international level. The practices look to move away from more traditional models of goalkeeper coaching and are based around many of the facets talked about in previous books – including skill acquisition, providing realistic match-specific environments, allowing for basic skill practice and technical formation, ensuring goalkeepers are trained to pick up relevant cues, triggers and information. These things translate directly to the game.

There are certain practices that are pitched at a lower, beginner level that are less 'chaotic' and which focus more on technical and physical basics.

Like all sections of this book, the practices are adaptable to those involved and should be tailored accordingly in terms of tempo, intensity, and coaching approach. A key aim of these practices is to set the scene to give goalkeepers a platform to find out what *works for them* to be effective as a goalkeeper; some techniques may not work for everyone, some physical movements may not work for everyone, and some tactical/positional approaches may not work for everyone. It's about being unique and individual as a goalkeeper; finding out what your key strengths are and maximising them through relevant and challenging training.

21

Practice Theme and Objectives: One touch passing incorporating handling techniques.

Number of GKs: 3-4.

Description: The GK plays a one-two pass from server 1 and turns to server 2 to perform the same action. They then face server 3 for a handling opportunity – this can be a volley or ground service. Rotate every four whole repetitions. Servers 1 and 2 are three yards away and server 3 is eight yards from the GK.

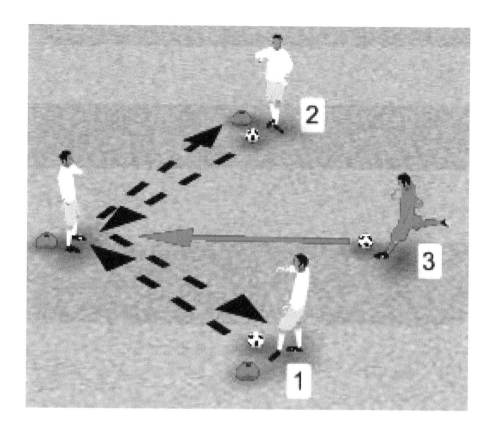

Goalkeeping Detail and Coaching Observations:

Focus on the body shape to play first time from all three GKs and that they co-ordinate their bodies fluently.

GK's hand position upon facing server 3.

General handling consistency, and moving body behind the ball, if service requires.

Lots of repetition to warm the feet and hands.

22

Practice Theme and Objectives: Handling and footwork.

Number of GKs: 3-5.

Description: The working GK receives a handling opportunity from server 1, secures the ball, and plays back with a pass from the ground. They will do the same from the other two servers whilst starting in a central position in a 4x4 yard grid. The GK will do this sequence twice before switching with another GK.

Goalkeeping Detail and Coaching Observations:

GK's set position upon server's ball contact.

Lots of repetition to warm the feet and hands.

Consistency of technical response to the ball.

Balance and control of body whilst travelling between servers – don't drop hands and keep upper body as still as possible.

23

Practice Theme and Objectives: Handling techniques and travelling over short distances.

Number of GKs: 3-4.

Description: The central server plays the ball towards the GK for a handling opportunity (ball 1). They then roll the ball to server 1 to control. The GK does the same onto the opposite side. They then travel to face server 1 who again gives them a handling opportunity. The GK then rolls the ball back to the central server. They do this again in the same way on the opposite side. This is one repetition at which point the GKs will rotate clockwise. The distance between the GK and all three servers can be different along with the handling opportunities presented to the working GK.

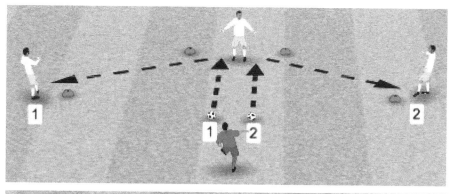

Goalkeeping Detail and Coaching Observations:

GK's set position upon server's ball contact.

Detail of throw to servers 1 and 2.

Lots of repetition to warm the feet and hands.

Consistency of technical response to the ball.

Balance and control of body whilst travelling between servers – don't drop hands and keep upper body as still as possible.

24

Practice Theme and Objectives: Footwork and co-ordination warm-up incorporating saving techniques.

Number of GKs: 2-4.

Description: The GK starts behind a set of six flat cones. The coach or server will call a number between one and six and, at this point, the GK will travel around this number of cones finishing in their starting position. They will then receive two handling opportunities from various ball positions. The GK can rotate after one set, or stay in for a longer period of time.

Goalkeeping Detail and Coaching Observations:

Speed to respond to the number called.

Control of body and limbs – lower body fast and co-ordinated, upper body steady and composed – don't drop hands.

Lots of repetition to warm the feet and hands.

Consistency of technical response to the ball.

25

Practice Theme and Objectives: Technical diving repetitions, and general handling.

Number of GKs: 2-4.

Description: The GK receives a one-step dive (progress a shift and dive) at a variable height. They throw the ball back to the server whilst on the ground and return to feet as quickly as possible, then travel around a cone to the side they've dived. They move to the middle of the grid for a handling opportunity from server 2. The GK can do different numbers of repetitions depending on the stage of the session and how physically ready they are.

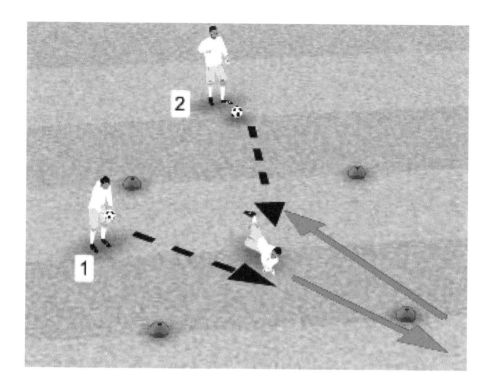

Goalkeeping Detail and Coaching Observations:

GK's ability to return to their feet as quickly as possible.

Good chance to work on different types of dive mechanics at different heights.

Observe GK's footwork patterns over different distances, and whether the stride pattern is appropriate.

Lots of handling repetitions.

Bring in random service from server 2 to include a decision-making aspect.

26

Practice Theme and Objectives: Footwork patterns and varied handling opportunities.

Number of GKs: 2-3.

Description: The GK starts in between two poles and receives a pass, handling opportunity, or a dive, from server 1. They then travel back and through the other two poles and receive the same from server 2. This is done two more times so the working GK receives six repetitions.

Goalkeeping Detail and Coaching Observations:

GK's set position at the time of the server's ball contact.

Lots of repetition to warm the feet and hands.

Consistency of technical response to the ball.

Focus on the ball and positioning of servers.

Balance and control of body whilst travelling between servers – don't drop hands and keep upper body as still as possible.

Bring in random service from server 2 to bring in a decision-making aspect.

27

Practice Theme and Objectives: Moving into line with balls and varying heights, and a focus on movement adaptability/athleticism.

Number of GKs: 2-6.

Description: Balls start in the centre of 10x10 yard grid with the coach. They serve a ball at either GK in grid 1 for them to claim the ball; that GK throws the ball to the other GK. The coach then turns to grid 2 and does exactly the same. The coach will then face the first grid again to receive the ball back to serve at either GK again and this process will continue. The GKs are travelling around their grids and transferring the ball between each other at all times. The two grids can have different service and return types from the GKs, to work on passing or throwing as well.

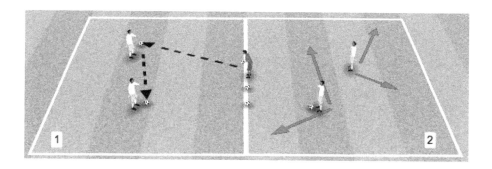

Goalkeeping Detail and Coaching Observations:

Efficiency of footwork to travel towards the coach's service.

Quality and consistency of actions in this warm-up practice.

Physical capability to perform 360-degree movements.

Progress the difficulty of the service to challenge the GKs.

28

Practice Theme and Objectives: Speed and reaction warm-up – cognitive and physical.

Number of GKs: 2-4.

Description: Each GK has a mannequin to defend from the coach who has a ball and is moving around the playing zone. They are looking to volley the ball from different angles and distances to beat the GKs. If the ball is blocked then secured, for example, that GK must distribute the ball into the two mini goals (pass, half volley, etc) and the coach will start with a new ball. The GKs or the coach can retrieve any loose balls in order to play on. To make this practice more challenging, the target the GKs are defending can be made bigger (e.g. two mannequins or a mini goal). For younger or novice GKs, this is a brilliant way to introduce blocking movements and to get them comfortable on when and how to use their legs to save the ball.

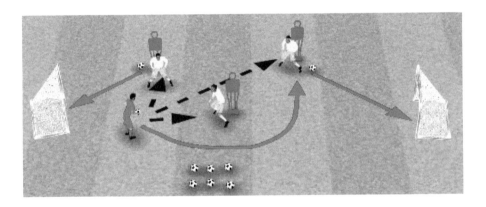

Goalkeeping Detail and Coaching Observations:

GKs' speed of limbs to repel/block the ball.

Posture and stance as the coach is moving around the playing zone – make sure GKs are in a position to move.

Concentration to follow the ball and pick the right time to execute movements.

Speed to pick up rebounds or loose balls.

The quality of any distribution methods used if the GK secures the ball.

29

Practice Theme and Objectives: Handling warm-up and short-range footwork patterns.

Number of GKs: 2-3.

Description: In picture 1, the working GK receives three separate serves in and around them at varying heights. In between each serve, they will roll the ball to the other GK to receive. After the three serves, the GK will drop off to the pole and receive the same three balls from the other GK. The distance in-between the servers and the GK can be increased and decreased. After this set, the GKs will rotate. If three GKs are participating, then have the third act as the first server. This practice has been used at elite level as a dynamic warm-up where the GKs can go through a range of different saving techniques which also incorporate movement and decision making.

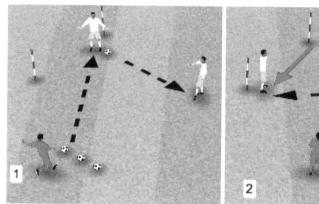

Goalkeeping Detail and Coaching Observations:

GK's set position upon the server's contact with the ball.

Lots of repetition to warm the feet and hands.

Consistency of technical response to the ball.

Focus on the ball and positioning of servers.

Balance and control of body whilst travelling between servers – don't drop hands and keep upper body as still as possible.

Bring in random service from both servers to include a decision-making aspect.

30

Practice Theme and Objectives: General physical warm-up incorporating hand and leg saves.

Number of GKs: 2-4.

Description: Server or coach has a ball at their feet dribbling within a pre-determined playing zone with high cones placed randomly around. The objective is for the GKs to stop the ball hitting the cones through blocking and repelling the ball away. Any loose balls can be picked up by the serving player to carry on the practice.

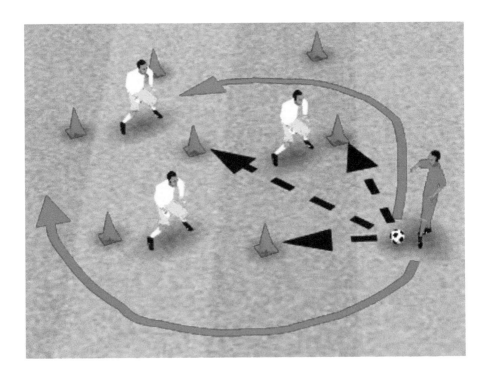

Goalkeeping Detail and Coaching Observations:

Ability to stay aware of ball positioning, and the different types of strikes from the server.

Speed of limbs to make contact with the ball (e.g. leg save or a dive).

The GK(s)' footwork to travel around the grid and make ground to save the ball.

31

Practice Theme and Objectives: Basic technical repetition including short footwork patterns.

Number of GKs: 1-3.

Description: The GK starts in front of the back cone and travels to the first line of cones to receive a ball from the server. They then drop off back to the cone and forward again to the opposite side for another ball from the server – if a GK is resting, they can act as server 2. Distance and the type of service can vary according to specific objectives.

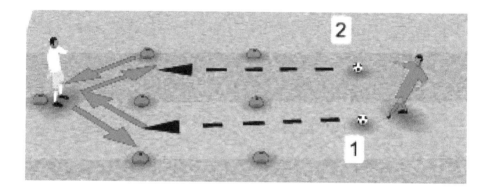

Goalkeeping Detail and Coaching Observations:

It is key that the GK keeps their feet as close to the ground whilst travelling as possible, and not be 'jumpy', as this is less efficient and causes the GK to be in the air.

Consistency and balance of set position.

GK's overall urgency and tempo for working at an intense level.

32

Practice Theme and Objectives: Judging the trajectory and flight of balls from different angles.

Number of GKs: 1-2.

Description: There is a box six yards in front of the GK and two yards outside of either post. The server will strike different types of volleys at the goal with the aim being to bounce the ball anywhere into the box. The server starts around 14 yards away from goal and can move anywhere around or behind the mannequins. The GK can also perform some kind of movement before the strike, e.g. drops off or springs forwards.

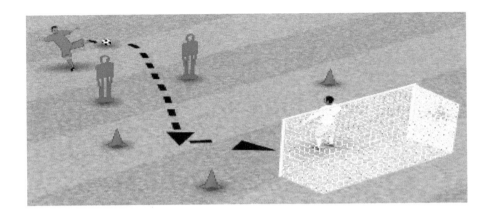

Goalkeeping Detail and Coaching Observations:

The GK's early assessment of the path of the ball. Can they be aggressive and keep the ball or do they need to stay deep and watch the ball/move laterally?

Execution of the technical response to the ball depending on the trajectory, direction, and pace of the ball.

Ideal for a warm-up practice before a main session to help the GK assess the moving ball early.

33

Practice Theme and Objectives: Technical repetition of different techniques from varying distances and angles.

Number of GKs: 3-4.

Description: The server or coach starts in a middle grid where three or four GKs have a set of four cones spread randomly around their own grid (this can vary in size but 10x10 yards is a good starting point). The server will take alternate turns in serving a ball to each GK who can be stood, ready, by any of their four cones. Once secured (if the ball is spilled this needs to be retrieved as quickly as possible), the GK then delivers the ball back to the server any way they wish. The GK will then jog to a different cone in their grid and the server will go to the next GK, and the sequence continues. If a ball is mis-hit, for example, the server has a pile of balls to start the practice again. GKs can move cones after each pre-determined number of repetitions to change the distances and angles of the service, and the service and direction of the serves to the GKs can vary. For younger GKs, this is a really good way to introduce new saving techniques as they will get lots of repetition of certain saves but with varying service types; the nature of delivery will make every ball played to them different in some way.

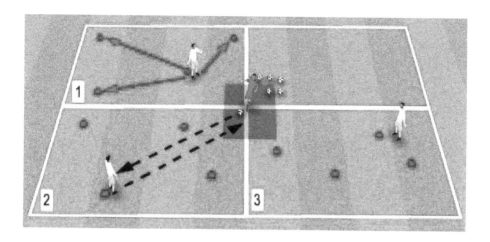

Goalkeeping Detail and Coaching Observations:

The individual's focus. With a quite a bit of activity occurring, can the GK(s) maintain focus on their own performance?

GK's response to balls and their movement. Use this practice as a chance for the GK to feel the ball and become physically active.

Change up the service as the practice continues to build in more decision-making opportunities.

34

Practice Theme and Objectives: Handling techniques and short/medium-range passing.

Number of GKs: 3-4.

Description: The balls start from the central server who strikes the ball towards the GK at any height to test their handling. The GK secures the ball, places the ball on the floor, and strikes towards either GK1 or GK2's goals to again test their handling. GKs 1 or 2 then roll the ball back to the central server. The practice continues for a number of pre-determined repetitions before the GKs rotate goals. The distances between each GK and the server can vary – six yards is a good starting range.

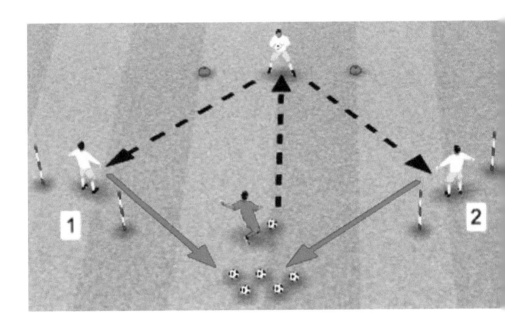

Goalkeeping Detail and Coaching Observations:

Initial footwork if the ball is outside the line of the GK's body.

Use this practice to warm-up the hands and feet, and focus on passing quality.

Build in more challenging and varied service as the practice progresses.

35

Practice Theme and Objectives: Receiving and passing over short distances and short-range shot stopping.

Number of GKs: 3-4.

Description: The balls start from the central server who plays into the GK. The GK can decide to play to either GK1 or GK2. The way they strike the ball into these GKs can vary, e.g. strike with laces towards the GK to test their handling. If GK1 or GK2 parries the ball back towards the first GK, they can look to score in either goal. If the GK secures the ball, they roll to the central server and the practice will begin again.

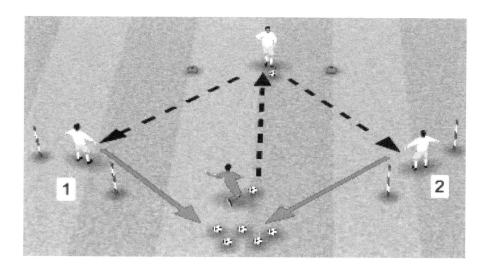

Goalkeeping Detail and Coaching Observations:

Body shape to play the way the GK has decided – the way they look to play will dictate their stance and touch.

Initial footwork if the ball is outside the line of the GK's body..

Build in more challenging and varied service as the practice progresses.

36

Practice Theme and Objectives: Receiving, passing, and general handling.

Number of GKs: 2-4.

Description: The ball starts with a wide server who passes the ball into the working GK. The GK receives and passes to server 1 who gives the GK a handling opportunity. The GK then rolls to server 2 (second diagram) to receive another random shot back at them. Each GK will then jog through to rotate.

Goalkeeping Detail and Coaching Observations:

Encourage consistency and detail for all actions – take every action on its own merits.

Even though more of a warm-up, the challenge nature of the shot from server 2 can be increased with them trying to score.

Observation on body co-ordination, balance, and control within the practice.

37

Practice Theme and Objectives: Lateral footwork and handling techniques.

Number of GKs: 3-4.

Description: The GKs start opposite the two servers at a pre-determined distance. The GKs will receive a ball and roll back to that server. The GKs will then cross-over, laterally, to the other server and this process will carry on. The distance between the lateral movements will be between three and six yards, and all GKs will rotate depending on the numbers working.

Goalkeeping Detail and Coaching Observations:

Set position focus following ball contact from the servers.

A focus on how efficient and co-ordinated the GKs movement patterns are.

Change the distance and type of service to breed new challenges.

38

Practice Theme and Objectives: Handling techniques with general movement patterns.

Number of GKs: 3-6.

Description: All GKs are working in a 10x10 square with one ball between them. They are throwing and catching the ball whilst moving around the square. At any point, server A (a coach or a GK) can call a GK to move into the 4-yard poled goal for a shot on this goal.

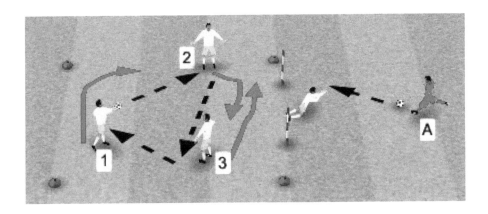

Goalkeeping Detail and Coaching Observations:

Consistency and detail of the GKs throwing and catching in the grid.

The speed with which the GK travels to the goal and their ability to decelerate.

Change server A's type of service.

Bring diving actions and jump mechanics into the grid work.

39

Practice Theme and Objectives: Diving actions and defending the goal.

Number of GKs: 1-3.

Description: Server 1 starts the practice by giving the GK a one-step dive on the angle – the GK will start in line with this ball. The GK will then return to their feet to roll the ball to server 2 who looks to score, first time, to the side upon which they dived. This is a great way to introduce reaction saves and techniques in the 4-8 yard range.

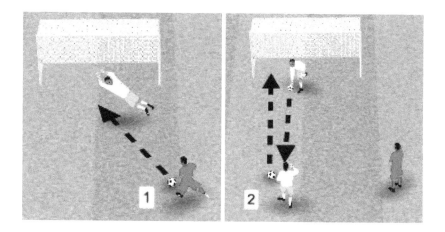

Goalkeeping Detail and Coaching Observations:

Diving shape and stance towards the height of the ball.

How the GK deals with the ball from a handling point of view – catch or deflect, etc.

The speed with which the GK can return to feet, to be in a position to produce a second diving action.

40

Practice Theme and Objectives: Footwork activation and handling warm-up.

Number of GKs: 2-3.

Description: The GK starts behind two mannequins. The coach will call left or right with the GK travelling in that direction around the mannequin to the middle. The central server will give the GK a one-two pass and the wide server will give the GK a random handling opportunity.

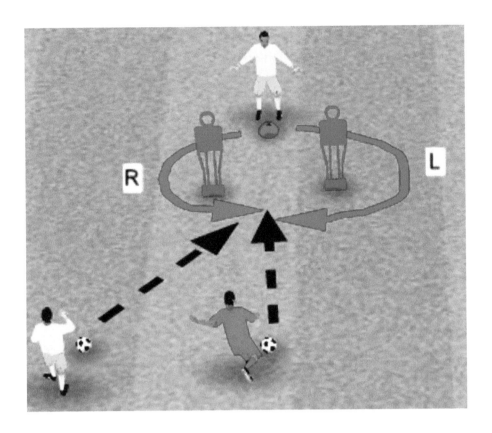

Goalkeeping Detail and Coaching Observations:

Balance and co-ordination of movement – short distance so keep hands close to the body.

Composure to deal with each ball on its merits.

Focus on the GK's set position in terms of being in an athletic position to move after travelling around the mannequin and changing directions.

41

Practice Theme and Objectives: Saving techniques within a 4-yard goal.

Number of GKs: 3.

Description: There is one ball in play at any point – any GK starts with the ball and rolls it out to the server. They can shoot at any goal they want. If the ball is secured, the GK rolls it back to the server and the practice continues. The distance between the goals can vary depending on the type of outcome required, e.g. if there is a 6-yard distance between the goals then 1v1 saves will be the main outcome. The serving player can move anywhere within the playing area. The practice can continue for a certain number of repetitions or be time limited.

Goalkeeping Detail and Coaching Observations:

GK's ability to maintain concentration throughout the practice.

Decision making relating to how to defend the goal – observe the GKs' use of the most effective body parts to make the save.

GK's positioning in relation to the moving ball, and if the central server changes their position.

42

Practice Theme and Objectives: Defending the goal – reaction saves and physical adaptation.

Number of GKs: 2-4.

Description: The ball starts from server 1 who gives the GK a strike in and around their body. The GK then rolls the ball back and, at this point, the server puts out an arm to the side of their body – the attacker will look to score to this side. The working GK can also decide to throw the ball out to an attacker for them to advance and shoot. Distances and the shooting angles between all servers can vary. Each GK will receive four repetitions before rotating. This practice has been used as part of an international warm-up as there is a big psychological element present; keepers respond to triggers in front of them alongside different saving situations.

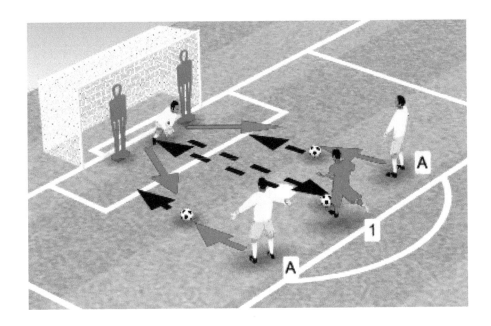

Goalkeeping Detail and Coaching Observations:

Speed in assessment and execution of the GK's response to the attacker's decision.

Desire to defend the goal.

Ability to produce 'unorthodox' movements and for the GKs to find their own individual styles to be effective.

43

Practice Theme and Objectives: Physical and technical adaptability around the goalmouth.

Number of GKs: 3-4.

Description: The ball starts from server 1 with the GK facing them. They play to the central server who gives the GK a ball to save between the mannequins. The ball is then returned to the central server with server 2 then attacking the goal to attempt to score – maximum three seconds. Players rotate every four repetitions and server 2's type of attempt on goal can vary as well. If the first ball is rebounded out, then any player can attempt to score.

Goalkeeping Detail and Coaching Observations:

Body control during the GK's travel from server 1's pass.

Speed in assessment and execution of the GK's response to the attacker's decision.

Desire to defend the goal.

Ability to produce 'unorthodox' movements and for the GKs to find their own individual styles to be effective.

44

Practice Theme and Objectives: Receiving and passing – incorporating general handling techniques.

Number of GKs: 3.

Description: The ball starts with server 1 who plays a pass to the GK. The GK then plays a one-two pass with server 2 before playing to server

3. Server 3 will then strike the ball at the GK for a handling opportunity. The distance between the players can vary depending on age/ability etc.

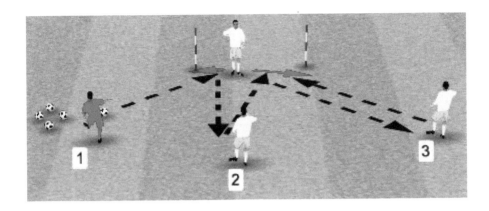

Goalkeeping Detail and Coaching Observations:

Passing and receiving detail, and adjusting to the player's position in order to pass.

Allow the GK to begin at their own pace to begin the warm-up process.

This is a good practice to work both passing and receiving with both feet, and also for working on a few different handling techniques.

45

Practice Theme and Objectives: Technical responses to different types of attempt on goal.

Number of GKs: 2-4.

Description: The ball starts from the wide server who strikes the ball at the GK. They travel across the goalmouth and throw to either server 1 or 2. They will take one touch and strike the ball back towards the GK. GKs will rotate every repetition with jogging and activation exercises between the changeover of serving positions to extend the warm-up.

Goalkeeping Detail and Coaching Observations:

Reading server 1 and 2's first touch – as the GK's throw will test their touch.

Work on different throws to activate the GK's upper body.

To progress the practices, change the positioning of the receiving players so their strikes on goal are from different angles and distances.

46

Practice Theme and Objectives: Bouncing ball judgement and jump mechanics – incorporating angled shot stopping.

Number of GKs: 2-4.

Description: Server 1 throws the ball anywhere into the shaded grid (10x12 shown) for the GK to claim – this could be a high or low bounce. The GK will then throw the ball out to server 2 who will take one touch and strike at goal. The servers in this diagram are 18-20 yards away from the goal posts.

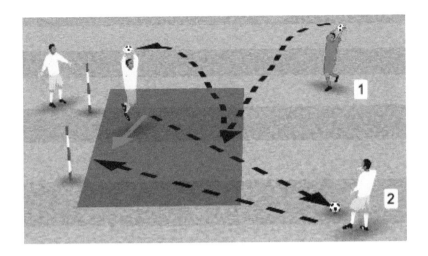

Goalkeeping Detail and Coaching Observations:

Focus on each GK's timing and assessment of their jump actions.

Use server 2's strike to work on catching and deflection handling detail.

Observe GKs' landing mechanics and their ability to get into a stable base position to deliver to server 2.

47

Practice Theme and Objectives: Dynamic warm-up featuring footwork patterns and handling.

Number of GKs: 2-6.

Description: The GK starts behind a set of cones with two more sets 4 yards between each other, in front of them. They perform any type of dynamic movement they want (skipping, jumping, hopping, quick feet, etc.) Then, receive a throw from the first server to volley pass back, then they travel laterally to face a handling opportunity from the next server.

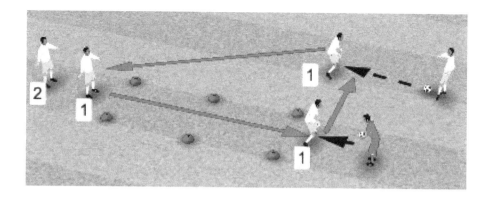

Goalkeeping Detail and Coaching Observations:

The movement section is a good opportunity to work on general co-ordination skills and body control.

Make the dynamic movements relevant to the session topic – e.g. include more bounding and jumping if crossing is the topic.

Change both servers' delivery to progress and vary the practice.

Increase the tempo of the service to gain some speed and agility outcomes.

48

Practice Theme and Objectives: Receiving and passing with basic crossing situations.

Number of GKs: 2-4.

Description: The GK starts with the ball at their feet playing a one-two pass with server 1. They will then switch the play towards server 2 giving them a pass they can gain control of (20-30 yards away to begin with). The GK will then travel to a position to defend the area from the crossed ball, and will deal with this cross how they see appropriate. To increase the difficulty, add pressure on the cross into the shaded zone.

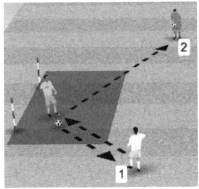 

Goalkeeping Detail and Coaching Observations:

The GK's position and body stance which will allow them to best play to server 2.

A good chance to work on different types of passes into the player.

Use server 2's cross as an opportunity to give the GK confidence in developing a provoking (front foot and positive) start position, and to defend the area with positivity and decisiveness.

49

Practice Theme and Objectives: Warm-up and activation grid – relevant GK actions and movement patterns.

Number of GKs: 2-6.

Description: Each GK will each have a ball in the 10x15 yard grid. In this grid, they will be performing dynamic mobility exercises and any stretches they want to do. There will be four stations that the GK can visit during this warm-up phase.

1. Volley or strike the ball into the mini goal and then retrieve.

2. Play the ball into the rebound board to control or catch.

3. Play the ball to the coach who will give a random handling opportunity.

4. Bounce a ball or throw the ball in the jump zone for jump mechanics.

This practice can be time led and altered to provide different elements to a warm-up such as diving, longer-range passes, and some more decision making situations.

Goalkeeping Detail and Coaching Observations:

Make sure GKs are performing movements correctly and safely.

Observe physical discrepancies (such landing instability, general co-ordination/balance and ability to adjust the body to moving balls) and encourage GKs to work both sides of the body at all times.

Consistency and detail here will set the tone to a session.

50

Practice Theme and Objectives: Technical repetitions warm-up.

Number of GKs: 2-4.

Description: The same practice will be happening either side of the goal (with the pole in-between as shown). If you have lower numbers of participants then the practice can take place with just one GK. Each working GK will receive 10 handling attempts from each ball position – 1, 2 or 3. If working in pairs, GKs will swap after each ball position and if three GKs are involved, they can rotate in a triangle with the coach serving. Service can be strikes, volleys, or half volleys in order for servers to get their lower limbs and kicking mechanics warm.

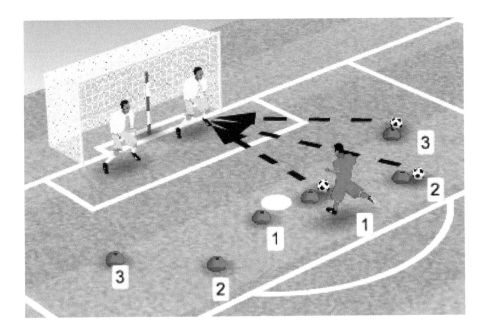

Goalkeeping Detail and Coaching Observations:

Opportunity to work on fundamental skills such as catching and being able to deal with attempts from varying heights.

If numbers don't allow, work from both sides and use one side of the goal.

Build in diving actions as the practice progresses.

51

Practice Theme and Objectives: Handling and diving repetitions.

Number of GKs: 3-4.

Description: The GK starts a yard behind a mannequin and, at their own pace, they travel around this mannequin to face the server. The server gives them a handling opportunity and the GK jogs back to go behind the mannequin. On the next repetition, the GK receives a diving save away from the middle of the practice. After these two repetitions, the GKs switch sides and perform the same again.

Goalkeeping Detail and Coaching Observations:

Good opportunity to work on the foundations of diving – both one and two-step dives.

To increase difficulty, make the first repetition random.

Use the changeover as a time to bring in some stretching and dynamic movements to continue the warm-up.

52

Practice Theme and Objectives: Medium-range passing – incorporating handling techniques.

Number of GKs: 3-4.

Description: The GK plays a one-two pass with server 1. They then receive a ball from server 3 from any position in a pre-positioned grid and will play off two touches to server 2 – who will be located in a wide position. This server will catch the ball and roll it towards server 3. Server 3 will receive the ball and shoot on goal after their first touch. This practice is a very good lead-up practice to a main shot stopping session; it allows the GKs to continue to get warm through passing and moving as well as having to deal with a shot on goal to finish with.

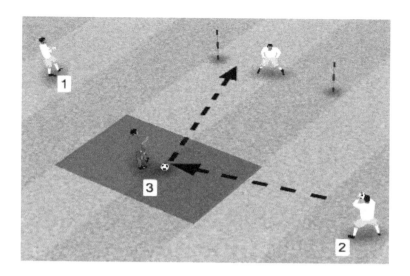

Goalkeeping Detail and Coaching Observations:

Passing and receiving detail – focus on the quality of any first touch to allow the GK to play with speed and composure.

GK reading the situation that may arise from server 2's square pass – can they engage the ball after server 3's first touch?

GK's general positioning and technical decision making from server 3's ball.

53

Practice Theme and Objectives: Medium-range passing – incorporating defending the goal.

Number of GKs: 3-5.

Description: The GK will receive the ball from server 1 just outside of the penalty area. They look to receive either side of the ball (see the two boxes in the 6-yard box) and play over the mannequin into server 2. Once this player has made connection with the ball, server 1 will play another ball towards server 3 who will look to score. This pass can be to server 3's feet or into space for a potential 1v1 situation. GKs will take four repetitions before rotating roles. Server 1 can either be a GK or the coach. This practice has been used at a high level with elite female GKs and provided them with an opportunity to combine two phases they'd been working on – playing into the full backs and defending through balls.

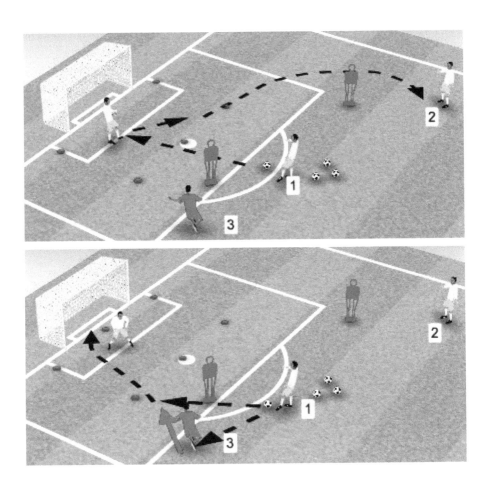

Goalkeeping Detail and Coaching Observations:

Receiving position and body shape from server 1 – does this allow them to play to server 2 with quality and composure? If pressure is added, think about supporting away from the pressure.

Detail whilst playing to server 2 – observe driven and/or clipped passes into the player.

Speed of the working GK to travel back across the goal mouth to respond to server 1's ball towards server 3.

GK's ability to assess server 3's attacking decision and their plan.

54

Practice Theme and Objectives: Handling techniques with a focus on fast decision making.

Number of GKs: 2-4.

Description: The GKs will be positioned in a 6x6 grid with six yards in-between them where the coach will be standing. The coach will deliver a ball for server 1 to deal with, and they will roll it back to coach. The coach will then deliver that same ball to GK2 and the process will continue. If a ball is spilled, the GK must respond appropriately (recover the ball or return to feet to drop off to defend the goal). Any balls that go away from the playing area will be left and the coach will use another. An example progression in this practice will be where, after GK1 secures the ball, they distribute directly to GK2 who will play the ball to the coach with the coach giving them another service to save.

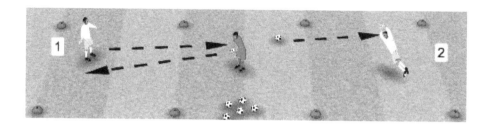

Goalkeeping Detail and Coaching Observations:

Movement and physical capabilities – move the GKs around the grid from the coach's service, to work on covering shorter distances.

Emphasise consistency and detail of catching, deflecting, and repelling the ball.

Make sure the GKs maintain awareness of the changes in service positions from the central server.

55

Practice Theme and Objectives: Travelling/covering the goal mouth while responding to different shot positions.

Number of GKs: 2-3.

Description: GK1 will face GK2; when GK 2 puts their arm out, GK1 will travel cross the goal. The attacker will be standing on a goal located in different positions from within the shaded grid area. The GK must match their footwork pattern to the position of the ball to best defend the goal as the attacker will try and score. Once familiar, the attacker will start two yards off the ball to bring in more decision making; further to this, they can take a touch before striking the ball.

Goalkeeping Detail and Coaching Observations:

When and how to set, after travelling across the goal.

Ability to scan for the ball positioning early, and to travel across/defend the goal accordingly.

Focus on the GK's ability to manoeuvre the ball away from GK2 and also the shooting player.

56

Practice Theme and Objectives: Jump mechanics and high ball assessment – incorporating shot stopping.

Number of GKs: 3-5.

Description: The working GK receives a high ball (throw or ground strike) from server 2 and, upon catching it, they throw to the central server. They do the same from server 3 then receive two attempts on goal from this central server, one after the other. A progression to work on different shot stopping angles would be for the central server to play the ball back to servers 2 and 3 to shoot at goal.

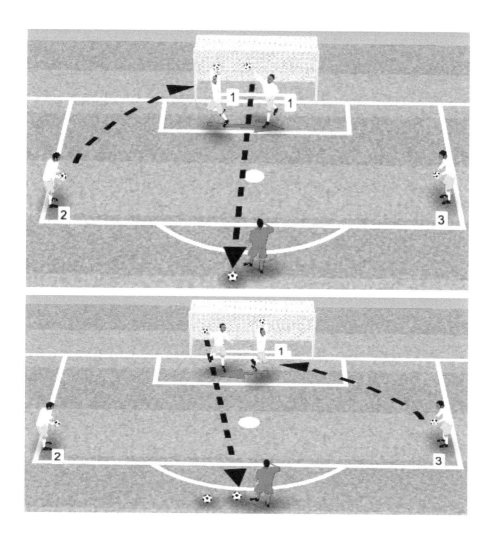

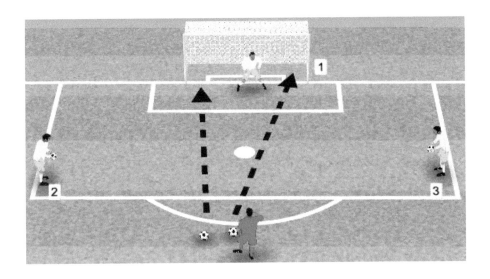

Goalkeeping Detail and Coaching Observations:

The timing and assessment of each jumping action – look at head and hand position along with how the GK uses their body to take off/generate power through the ball.

Observe the GK's landing process – make sure it's safe and uses two feet, then assess the GK's ability to transfer the ball to the central server.

Use the throwing section to work on both arms and different types of throw.

General shot stopping observation – positioning, ball assessment, and technical execution of techniques.

57

Practice Theme and Objectives: Passing and ball control – incorporating shot stopping.

Number of GKs: 3-4.

Description: GK (marked as B) plays a ball into GKC from one of the three ball positions. This ball will be in the air towards GKC who has to control the ball to allow the attacker to shoot first time on goal against GKA. Players will rotate every six repetitions, with GKB taking their pass into GKC from any ball (shown as 1, 2 and 3); GKC can position themselves anywhere within the playing area.

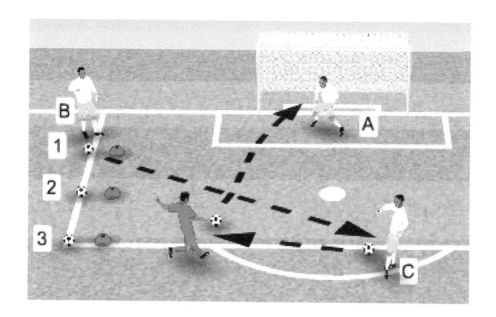

Goalkeeping Detail and Coaching Observations:

GKB's passing quality and accuracy to allow GKC to set the ball first time – this will dictate the quality of the repetition.

GKC's weight of touch and ability to assess the pass and move accordingly.

GKA's assessment of this first touch (can they intercept and engage the ball) or do they need to defend the goal, putting emphasis on the attacking player?

Any recovery or second save opportunities that GKA may receive.

Build in a competition where each GK defends the goal for three sets of five repetitions.

58

Practice Theme and Objectives: General handling techniques.

Number of GKs: 4-6.

Description: The practice will be the same for both sides – the server touches around the mannequin and gives the GK a catch (in and around their body). GK1 then throws the ball to server 3 for them to attempt to score after one touch. GK2 then does the same after GK1 has completed their repetition. The first servers can act as rebound players as well.

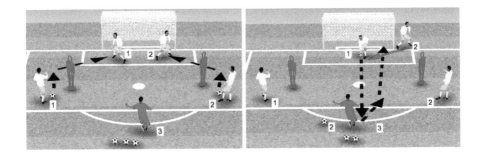

Goalkeeping Detail and Coaching Observations:

Make sure the service from the starting players is of good quality so the practice can flow smoothly.

GK1's ability to release the ball with speed and quality to server 3.

GK2's response to the conclusion of GK1's repetition; they need to be aware when they can move into the goal.

Both GKs desire to defend the goal and respond to the changing position of the ball and shooting triggers (e.g. has the attacking player secured possession?).

59

Practice Theme and Objectives: Distribution methods – incorporating defending the goal.

Number of GKs: 4-6.

Description: The GKs will be numbered and start outside the posts of a mini pitch – 15x25 yards – with the ball starting centrally with the coach. The coach calls a number and a distribution method, e.g. "1. Half volley". This pair of GKs, and the called distribution method, will be used in this repetition. The coach can play the ball into either half of the pitch and, if the ball is secured, that GK can then carry on the practice with that distribution method. Each GK can use the whole of their half and the ball is in play until either a goal has been scored or the ball goes out of the grid. This practice acts as a good way to finish a distribution session as it allows GKs to practice their variations in a less isolated environment; also, some shot stopping is built in.

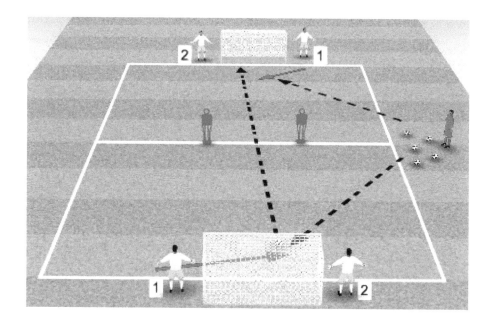

Goalkeeping Detail and Coaching Observations:

Quality and consistency of distribution methods.

Use this as a playground to try new techniques (feet and hands/left and right sides).

GK's ability to defend the goal and not give up on any attempts, no matter what the range or situation.

Build in a competition and encourage distribution from different angles, e.g. the coach plays the ball into the grid in different spaces and GKs must play the ball where it lies.

60

Practice Theme and Objectives: Defending the area or the goal from central positions.

Number of GKs: 3-6.

Description: Two GKs start in-between the width of the goal, with the other participants travelling around the shaded grid with a ball each. The coach will call a number and at this point that GK will stay in the goal to face an attempt on goal from any attacker. The other GK gets out of the way as quickly as possible. Any rebounds can be retrieved by any attacker in the practice to continue the repetition.

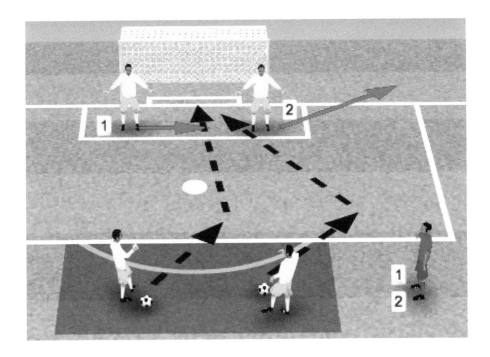

Goalkeeping Detail and Coaching Observations:

How does the GK respond to the attacker's approach to goal? Is their technical response appropriate, e.g. 1v1 save technique vs long-range shot stopping.

Bring in mannequins to introduce visual obstructions.

How does the GK react to recovery and second save situations?

61

Practice Theme and Objectives: Speed and mobility warm-up focusing on diving actions.

Number of GKs: 2-4.

Description: GKs start outside the posts and begin to gain momentum before the coach throws the ball at different heights towards the side of the goal which the GK is travelling. Once a GK has made contact on the ball, the next GK goes from the post that the first GK has dived towards and performs the same as the previous GK. As a progression, the throw can be in the direction the GK is travelling from, so they have to quickly readjust their body.

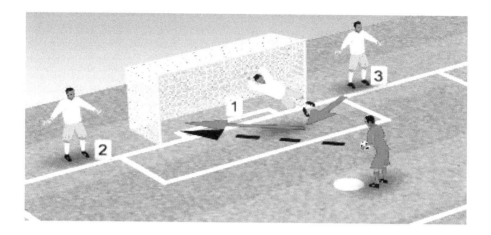

Goalkeeping Detail and Coaching Observations:

Ability of the GK to co-ordinate their footwork to push off to dive whilst in motion.

Bring in bottom vs top hand saves during the practice.

Emphasise the need for GKs to extend their arms and to get their heads as close to the ball as possible, to increase their dive range.

62

Practice Theme and Objectives: Handling opportunities with a 'set position' focus.

Number of GKs: 1-4.

Description: Each GK has a 4x4 yard grid to stay in for this practice. The server will move across the line giving each GK a serve anywhere in the grid – the server can be any distance away but 6 yards is a good starting point. To return the ball, the GK must roll the ball back so it lands in the opposite grid that the serve was taken from – with the final position of the ball being the position the server will strike from. The server will strike at all three GKs then return to the beginning.

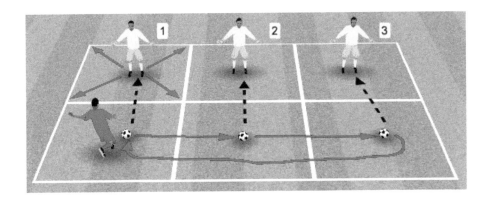

Goalkeeping Detail and Coaching Observations:

Emphasise clean handling and moving feet to get behind the ball.

Make sure the weight of the throw, back to the server, allows them to play the ball back upon their next repetition.

Build in diving actions, and also a competition, making the line behind the GKs mini goals.

63

Practice Theme and Objectives: Footwork activation and general handling.

Number of GKs: 2-6.

Description: An 8x8 yard grid will be surrounded by various footwork obstacles (hurdles, cones. and a ladder, as shown). The GKs perform these movements whenever they want and can use the grid for static and dynamic stretching and to receive a ball from the coach to get their hands warm.

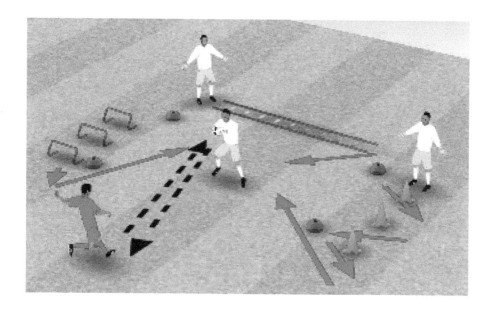

Goalkeeping Detail and Coaching Observations:

Make sure GKs are performing movements correctly and safely.

Observe any physical discrepancies (such landing instability, general co-ordination/balance and ability to adjust the body to moving balls) and encourage GKs to work both sides of the body at all times.

Consistency and detail here will set the tone to a session.

Handling and technical consistency when receiving a strike from the coach.

64

Practice Theme and Objectives: Footwork activation and general handling.

Number of GKs: 2-4.

Description: The working GK starts behind a series of footwork obstacles (hurdles shown). They complete this and receive a ball from GK2 which they play into the central server. The GK then travels towards the cone to receive a ball from the server. If more than one GK is working, the other GK should start his repetition exactly when the first GK completes his repetition. A practice such as this is an effective lead in session after a general warm-up, and before a more advanced handling session.

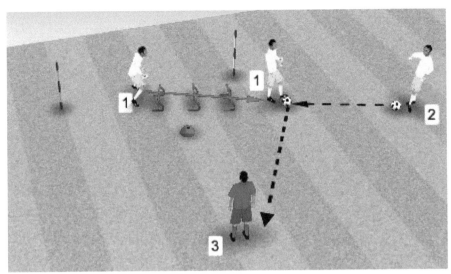

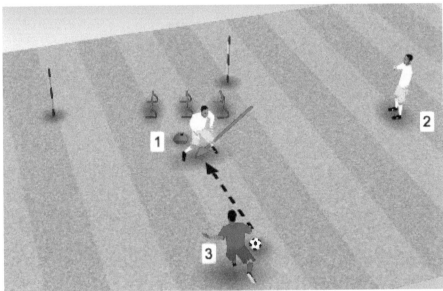

Goalkeeping Detail and Coaching Observations:

GK's co-ordination and power generation from the hurdles or any kind of footwork obstacle.

Balance to receive and play with quality and purpose to server 3.

Use the strike from server 3 to go through different handling techniques and ranges(s).

65

Practice Theme and Objectives: General handling – incorporating speed and agility.

Number of GKs: 4-6.

Description: This exercise is for a pair of GKs, in two 6x6 yard grids, either side of a goal appropriate to the age/ability of the GKs. These GKs are throwing the ball to each other whilst moving around their grid. The coach will call either A or B – corresponding to the grid – and the GK who has the ball at that moment in time will throw or pass the ball to a central server (can be the coach) and travel as fast as possible to defend the goal. As soon as the central player receives the ball, they can shoot at goal. Once this ball has been dealt with, the practice will start again.

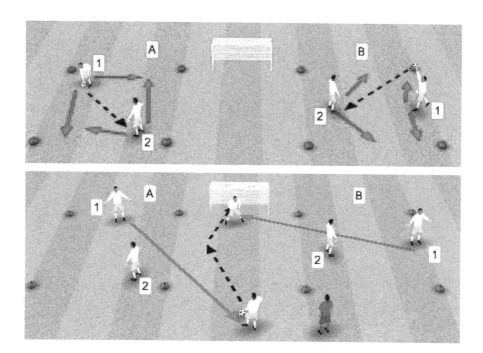

Goalkeeping Detail and Coaching Observations

Quality of throwing and catching within each grid.

The accuracy and playability of the distribution to the central server.

Build in a competition between both grids; whoever concedes the fewest number of goals wins.

Assess the method and speed of travel from the grids to defend the goal – look at the depth the GKs have, in relation to the goal.

Decision making with regard to the GK's technical responses to the attempts on goal.

66

Practice Theme and Objectives: General handling – incorporating speed and agility.

Number of GKs: 4-6.

Description: This exercise is for a pair of GKs, in two 6x6 yard grids, either side of a goal appropriate to the age/ability of the GKs. These GKs are throwing the ball to each other whilst moving around their grid. The coach will call either A or B corresponding to the grid – the GK who has the ball at that moment in time will throw or pass the ball to a central server (can be the coach) and travel as fast as possible to defend the goal. Each grid has their *own* goal to defend and, if the ball is rebounded out, the non-working GK can look to score against the other grid's GK. This practice has been used to great effect with younger GKs to work on their concentration and awareness.

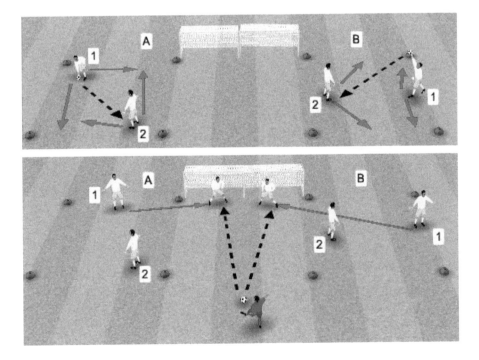

Goalkeeping Detail and Coaching Observations:

Quality of throwing and catching within each grid.

Build in a competition between both grids; whoever concedes the fewest number of goals wins.

Assess the method and speed of travel from the grids to defend the goal – look at the depth the GKs have, in relation to the goal.

Decision making with regard to the GK's technical responses to the attempts on goal.

67

Practice Theme and Objectives: Short footwork patterns with general handling.

Number of GKs: 3-4.

Description: GK receives a ball from server 1 to catch and roll ball to the server. Server 1 will point either side and the GK will travel to defend the goal on the angle from GK2 or GK3's strike on goal. The working GK will have five repetitions before players rotate roles.

Goalkeeping Detail and Coaching Observations:

GK's ability to travel from goal to goal with composure and control of their body.

Observation with regard to general catching and hand shapes.

Build in a more testing service from servers 2 and 3 as the practice progresses.

68

Practice Theme and Objectives: Handling and diving warm-up.

Number of GKs: 3-4.

Description: Two servers on the edge of the box in a central position with two GKs on an angle. The servers play a one-two pass with the GKs and look to play the ball towards the same side that they are positioned. The working GK will receive three balls from each side before players rotate. Servers and GKs can swap roles with the GKs offering the strike at goal. The second phase of the practice sees whether the server can strike the ball to either side of the working GK.

Goalkeeping Detail and Coaching Observations:

GK's ability to shift laterally and get set for the strike.

This exercise offers good opportunities to bring in coaching points such as attacking the ball and getting the GK's head as close to the ball as possible. Progress the GK's to random service, after a familiarisation warm-up.

69

Practice Theme and Objectives: Handling and diving warm-up.

Number of GKs: 2.

Description: The ball will start with the central server who plays into GK1. They control the ball and strike towards the goal giving GK2 a diving save (heights can vary or be random depending on time available in the session). If GK2 secures the ball, they will roll to the server to give GK1 the same action that they received. If the ball goes wide, the server will start with the ball and play back to the GK who received the previous ball. This is a good exercise before a main shot stopping practice.

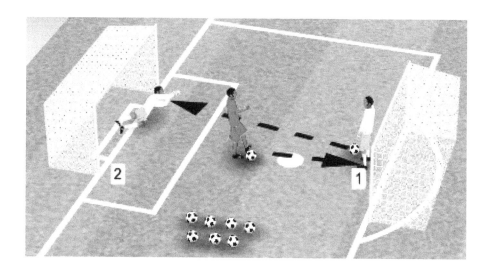

Goalkeeping Detail and Coaching Observations:

Increase the pace and tempo of the practice as it continues.

This exercise can also be used for work on defending the goal and making recovery saves.

Observations on footwork to cover the goal, and to gain momentum on diving actions, will be crucial.

GK's ability to assess different types of ball trajectories is central to success, as well as their ability to select a technical response according to the specific ball.

70

Practice Theme and Objectives: Passing and receiving warm-up – with a focus on different passing ranges.

Number of GKs: 2-4.

Description: GK1 starts with the ball facing the server. They play the ball into the server and receive it back at different angles and weights of pass. The GK must decide whether to play first time (slower ball and opportunity to adjust body position) or take a touch when faster paced balls are received. The GK will then play to GK2 and the same process will begin. The third picture shows what this could look like with three GKs working together. This practice acts as a good starting point before a specific tactical distribution session.

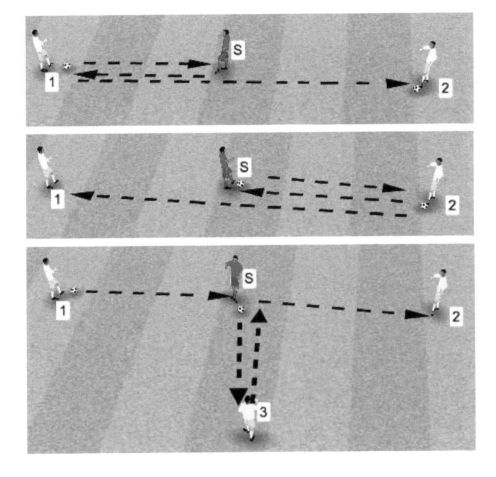

Goalkeeping Detail and Coaching Observations:

Opportunity to work on different techniques and different passing ranges.

Ability of the GKs to assess when and how to play first or second time.

Add pressure from the server after their initial pass.

Focus on using both feet to control, manoeuvre, and pass the ball.

71

Practice Theme and Objectives: Striker and ball assessment visual warm-up

Number of GKs: 3-5.

Description: Two servers (could be more) are positioned anywhere outside the penalty area. Behind the goal, there will be a server with coloured cones. The servers will have a designated colour and when this colour is held up, that server will touch out of their feet and shoot on goal. The GK will obviously be facing the play so won't see these coloured cones.

Goalkeeping Detail and Coaching Observations:

Speed of assessing the specific ball that gets struck at goal.

General shot stopping principles such as positioning, set position, and technical response from the GK.

Use this practice as an opportunity to work on parry/deflection/repel safety zones, from initial shots on goal.

Add more servers and/or a pass before the strike on goal to change the picture and visual cues available to the GK.

Team-Based Goalkeeper Practices

This third section of the book will cover practices involving the goalkeeper and outfield players – from either an attacking or defensive point of view.

Training in isolation (either as an individual or as a group) has many developmental benefits for goalkeepers; these upcoming practices look to add in game-realistic factors such as multiple attempts on goal, different starting points for attack, different finishing angles and distances, blocked vision for the GKs, moving balls, and defensive communication, to name but a few. The participants in GK-specific sessions often like to think of themselves as closet Lionel Messis or Cristiano Ronaldos!

So, by having the real article in the form of outfield players who regularly practise crossing, finishing, through balls, and movement patterns, the challenge and quality of the sessions is raised. Now, these practices can be viewed from two different angles – the GK coach running the session with outfield players supplementing things, or the GK being a focal point within an outfield session that's led by the head coach. Both of these approaches can be catered for in these practices.

The main focus is not just on the GKs and involving the attackers just to shoot at them. Nor is it the opposite (where GKs are just used as a body for attacking players to fire shots at). No, the aim is always to have 'outcomes' and a realistic practice environment. In turn, it's important, from a GK's point of view, that they're valued by the whole team and staff; making them a focal point in any team session can help breed this.

72

Goalkeeping Themes: Finishing with attackers – from wide angles.

Practice Objectives: To give the GK work on attempts on goal from different angles, distances, bouncing balls, and approaches, from 12+ yards. To give the attacking players work on receiving skills and different types of finishing techniques (coaches should be looking at their ability to get shots off quickly, but with quality).

Description: The ball starts from server 1 who strikes the ball into the GK. The GK then throws to either server 2 or 3 (throw inside the mannequin to a player) with them taking a touch outside the mannequin before striking at goal. The GK can throw the ball at any height or pace to the attacker to test their receiving skills. The opposite server can look for rebounds and can work on the timing of their movement. The three attackers can rotate to work on both feet and different angles.

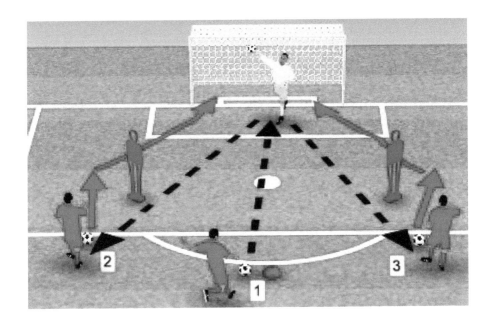

Progressions:

The GK can side-volley or pass the ball to servers 2 and 3 (or go for random distribution).

Servers 2 and 3, upon receiving the ball, can provide a first-time touch into the path of server 1 who can have a first-time attempt on goal.

Servers 2 and 3 can finish how they want (unlimited touches, etc.) to bring in 1v1 situations.

GK Learning Detail:

Technical: Distribution accuracy and overall technique | Ability to manoeuvre the ball away from immediate danger (hand shapes based upon the pace of the ball)

Tactical: Positioning of the attackers first touch – controlled touch, loose ball, or bouncing ball | Ability to deal with any second phase situations such as a cut back, a second attempt on goal, or engaging the ball to block/smother | A key observation will be on how wide the first touch takes the attacker in relation to the goal

Psychological: Assessment of the attacker's first touch and the GK's position based upon the ball (think about left foot vs right foot) | Appropriateness of save selection

Physical: Set position and balance upon the attacker's strike on goal | General speed and agility to change position quickly to respond to the movement of the ball

Social/Environmental: If there are two GKs working, build in some challenges (e.g. a point scoring system) | Change the positioning of the attackers, and also distances, to alter the challenges the GK will face

Outfield Learning Detail:

Technical: Quality of first touch to move away from a mannequin and strike on goal off their second touch | Consistency and detail of their technical proficiency

Tactical: Type of finishing required in accordance with where their first touch takes them in relation to the goal

Psychological: Assessment of where the GK is positioned | Decision of how to strike the ball – laces, side foot, elevation, pace, and precision | Desire to score and the confidence to try a variety of finishing types

Physical: Body shape, balance, and co-ordination whilst striking | Observation of non-kicking foot and follow-through

Social/Environmental: Place emphasis on the attacking players playing at match tempo/intensity and being ruthless in front of goal – they should try to score at every attempt

73

Goalkeeping Themes: Combination plays from around the penalty box – different types of entries and approaches.

Practice Objectives: To work the GK on attempts on goal from different angles, distances, bouncing balls, and approaches from 12+ yards. To give the attacking players work on receiving skills and different types of finishing technique. To give midfield players work on quick combination play around the penalty box.

Description: Servers 1 and 2 are passing in a 10x10-yard grid; at any point, either server can look to play to servers 3 or 4 for them to finish on goal. The opposite server can look for rebounds and can work on the timing of their movement. The four attackers can rotate to work on both feet and different angles.

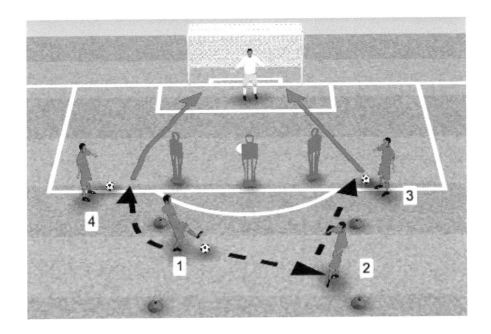

Progressions:

Change the initial grid size to open up different angles for through balls/combination play.

Build in touch or time limits.

Allow attackers to finish 1v1.

GK Learning Detail:

Technical: Technical response based upon the finishing range (1v1, short or longer-range strike) | Ability to manoeuvre the ball away from immediate danger (hand shapes based upon the pace of the ball)

Tactical: Positioning of the attackers first touch – controlled touch, loose ball, or bouncing ball | Ability to deal with any second phase situations such as a cut back, a second attempt on goal, or engaging the ball to block/smother | A key observation will be on how wide the first touch takes the attacker in relation to the goal

Psychological: Assessment of the attacker's first touch and the GK's position based upon the ball – think about left foot vs right foot |

Appropriateness of save selection | Decision on when, where, and how to engage the ball

Physical: Set position and balance upon the attacker's strike on goal | General speed and agility to change position quickly to respond to the movement of the ball | Ability to show an appropriate body position if engaging the ball for a 1v1 save

Social/Environmental: If there are two GKs working, build in some challenges e.g. points scoring system | Change the positioning of the attackers, and also distances, to alter the challenges the GK will face | Focus on consistency of actions and appropriateness of decision making

Outfield Learning Detail:

Technical: The weight and accuracy of the midfielders' passing, combination play, and through balls | Quality of first touch to move away from a mannequin and strike on goal off their second touch | Consistency and detail of their technical proficiency

Tactical: Type of finishing required, in accordance to where their first touch takes them, in relation to the goal

Psychological: Assessment of where the GK is positioned | Decision of how to strike the ball – laces, side foot, elevation, pace, and precision | Desire to score and the confidence to try a variety of finishing types

Physical: Body shape, balance, and co-ordination whilst striking | Observation of non-kicking foot and follow through

Social/Environmental: Place emphasis on the attacking players playing at match tempo/intensity and being ruthless in front of goal – trying to score at every attempt

74

Goalkeeping Themes: Short and long-range saving techniques.

Practice Objectives: To provide a multiple outcome practice that encompasses both technical and physical elements – the GKs will have to assess the relevant cues to respond to a changing environment. For attacking players, a main objective will be to work on longer-range shooting techniques.

Description: GKs 1 and 2 both start with a football and just outside either post. GK1 throws the ball to the coach/server who is holding a hand-held rebound net. GK1 will follow their throw and receive the ball from the net and attempt to keep the ball out of the goal. GK2 will then do the same thing from the opposite side (at this point. the practice can enter phase two or both GKs will get another repetition).

The second phase will consist of the server/coach calling out attacker A or B (and moving out of the playing area). That attacker will have the choice of shooting first time or playing a through ball or a pass to the opposite attacker. If the second option is performed, then this attacker has one touch before shooting. Any balls that are left in the immediate playing area can be rebounded to bring in recovery saves or to defend the goal.

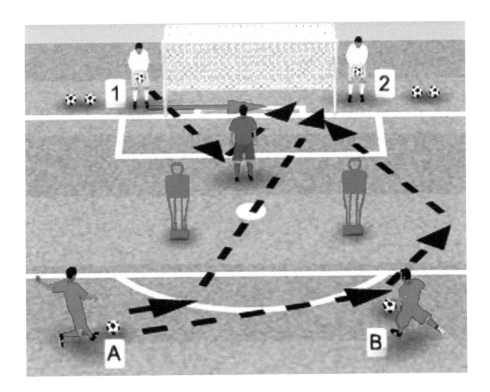

Progressions:

The receiving attacker can travel towards goal for a 1v1 scenario.

Change the position of the attacking players (if more than two, factor these positions in).

GK Learning Detail:

Technical: Within phase 1, the choice of body part to use – the speed of the ball from the rebound net will dictate the best option | Technical response based upon the finishing range (1v1, short, or longer-range strike) | Ability to manoeuvre the ball away from immediate danger (hand shapes based upon the pace of the ball)

Tactical: A key observation will be on how wide the first touch takes the attacker in relation to the goal | Depth in the goalmouth | Ability to deal with any second phase situations such as a cut back, a second attempt on goal, or engaging the ball to block/smother

Psychological: Assessment of the attacker's first touch and the GK's position on the ball – think about left foot vs right foot | Appropriateness of save selection | Decision on when, where, and how to engage the ball

Physical: Speed and power within the first phase | Flexibility and adaptability of limbs in the first phase | Set position and balance upon the attacker's strike on goal | General speed and agility to change position quickly to respond to the movement of the ball | Ability to show an appropriate body position if engaging the ball for a 1v1 save

Social/Environmental: If there are two GKs working, build in some challenges e.g. points scoring system | Change the positioning of the attackers, and also distances, to alter the challenges the GK will face | Focus on consistency of actions and appropriateness of decision making

Outfield Learning Detail:

Technical: The weight and accuracy of the midfielders' passing, combination play, and through balls | Quality of first touch to move away from a mannequin and strike on goal off their second touch | Consistency and detail of their technical proficiency

Tactical: Type of finishing required in accordance to where their first touch takes them in relation to the goal

Psychological: Assessment of where the GK is positioned | Decision of how to strike the ball – laces, side foot, elevation, pace, and precision | Desire to score and the confidence to try a variety of finishing types

Physical: Body shape, balance, and co-ordination whilst striking | Observation of non-kicking foot and follow through

Social/Environmental: Place emphasis on the attacking players playing at match tempo/intensity and being ruthless in front of goal – trying to score at every attempt

75

Goalkeeping Themes: Defending the area, or the goal, during combination play.

Practice Objectives: To give the GK practice in deciding whether to engage the ball or to defend the goal. This initial decision will dictate how they look to save the ball. For the attackers, the main aims will be to penetrate with quality and efficiency through quick movements of the ball and to be creative. For the defender, they will work with the GK to try and stop the attackers scoring.

Description: The ball starts with the GK. They can distribute how they like to either side's attacking player (1 or 2). The receiving player and player 3 look to score within four seconds through any way they can. The offside law is in operation. To stop them, there will be a defender – if they intercept the ball, they look to play to the non-used attacker.

After the initial four seconds, if the ball has been shot at goal and saved, the practice can continue to incorporate rebounds and a second phase.

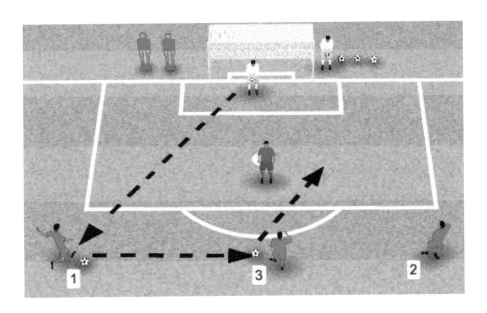

Progressions:

Change the positions of all attacking players (angles from goal and also distances).

Alter the time allowed for the attacking players – and bring on some mannequins as obstacles.

Build-in wide players for cutbacks and balls across the face of the box.

GK Learning Detail:

Technical: Distribution accuracy and playability of the pass | Technical response based upon the finishing range (1v1, short, or longer-range strike) | Ability to manoeuvre the ball away from immediate danger (hand shapes based upon the pace of the ball) | How the GK is able to adapt their technical response in relation to the picture in front of them

Tactical: Information to the defender | GK's initial position after their distribution – defend the area first | When to vacate the goal to engage the ball – what are the triggers to do this? | General positioning based upon the picture that's in front of them

Psychological: Assessment of the attacker's first touch and the direction/weight of this touch| Appropriateness of save selection | Decision on when, where, and how to engage the ball | The speed of the assessment and execution of all actions from the GK

Physical: Ability to move with speed and control, to defend the area initially from the combination play | Set position and balance upon the attacker's strike on goal | General speed and agility to change position quickly to respond to the movement of the ball | Ability to show an appropriate body position if engaging the ball for a 1v1 save

Social/Environmental: If there are two GKs working, build in some challenges, e.g. point scoring system | Change the positioning of the attackers – and also distances – to alter the challenges the GK will face | Focus on consistency of actions and appropriateness of decision making | The attackers are overloaded so expect them to have success

Outfield Learning Detail:

Technical: The weight and accuracy of passing, combination play, and through balls | Consistency and detail of their technical proficiency | Encourage different types of finish

Tactical: Encourage the early shot if the goal opens up | Type of finishing required in accordance to where their first touch takes them in relation to the goal | If the wide attacking player is forced wide of the goal, defend on the inside to block any shots or square balls

Psychological: Look to attack in different directions to draw the defender out or away from protecting the goal | The ball is the priority for the defender and to delay and dictate the attacking pattern of play

Physical: Snap shots with no backlift – especially if the defender is engaging the ball as the GK may be caught moving or off-guard | Speed of movement and front foot mentality | General balance and co-ordination to strike the ball first time or whilst body is in motion | Deceleration of defender and their posture/stance

Social/Environmental: Place emphasis on the attacking players playing at match tempo/intensity and being ruthless in front of goal – trying to score at every attempt

76

Goalkeeping Themes: Defending the goal – quick changes of ball movement and attempts on goal through bodies.

Practice Objectives: To provide the GK with opportunities to focus on their ability to respond to quick changes of ball direction along with their lateral movement across the goal. For the attacking players, the emphasis will be on their first touch, allowing them to manipulate the ball into a shooting opportunity off that initial contact.

Description: The ball starts with attacker 1 who is in a central position. They play a randomly weighted pass against a rebound board (or an equivalent piece of equipment) with this pass either allowing attacker 1 to shoot from ball position 2, or the ball going across to attacker 3 who can shoot first time or take a touch to move the ball (all of this at high speed due to the position on the pitch). Rebound situations are encouraged and if the GK secures the ball, a distribution target can be put outside the shown playing area.

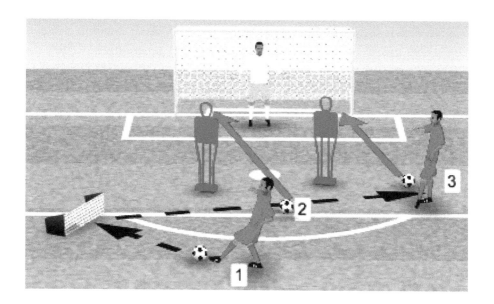

Progressions:

Change the position and angle of the rebound board.

Change the position of the second attacker.

Allow the second attacker to advance towards the goal for a 1v1 situation.

GK Learning Detail:

Technical: Ability to manoeuvre the ball away from immediate danger (hand shapes based upon the pace of the ball) | Distribution accuracy and overall technique

Tactical: Positioning of the attacker's first touch – controlled touch, loose ball, or bouncing ball | Ability to deal with any second phase situations such as a cut back, a second attempt on goal, or engaging the ball to block/smother | A key observation will be on how wide the first touch takes attacker 2 in relation to the goal | GK's depth in the goal from longer-range attempts

Psychological: Assessment of the attacker's first touch and the decision relating to the GK's position based upon the ball – think about left foot vs right foot | Appropriateness of save selection

Physical: Set position and balance upon the attacker's strike on goal | General speed and agility to change position quickly to respond to the movement of the ball

Social/Environmental: If there are two GKs working, build in some challenges, e.g. point scoring system | Change the positioning of the attackers – and also distances – to alter the challenges the GK will face | Focus on consistency of actions and appropriateness of decision making | The attackers are overloaded so expect them to have success

Outfield Learning Detail:

Technical: The weight and accuracy of passing, combination play, and through balls | Consistency and detail of players' technical proficiency | Encourage different types of finishes

Tactical: Assess the GK's position in the goal as this can dictate the attackers' decision on how to strike the ball | Look to play away from mannequins to create new space and angles to finish

Psychological: Confidence to try new techniques | Quick decisions on what to do with the ball – have a plan and be pro-active

Physical: Snap shots with no back lift (as the GK may be caught moving or off-guard) | Speed of movement and front foot mentality | General balance and co-ordination to strike the ball first time or whilst body is in motion

Social/Environmental: Place emphasis on the attacking players playing at match tempo/intensity and being ruthless in front of goal – trying to score at every attempt

77

Goalkeeping Themes: General shot stopping from different distances.

Practice Objectives: To give GKs repeated exposure to shot stopping scenarios in a fluid environment. For the attacking players, it's a chance to work on different types of finish – both with the ball and moving onto a passed ball.

Description: Either GK will start with the ball (in this practice, the GK will alternate to start each repetition). They roll out to either Attacker 1 or 2 who takes a touch forwards and strikes at goal. The receiving player also has the option of playing in the opposite attacker for a first-time strike on goal. The process will then start again from the other GK. The distance between the goals and the width of the attackers will dictate the type of outcomes – think about what each player's individual needs are, and what specific outcome is needed. In the below diagrams, one goal has mannequins around it to add chaos and the other is clear – which can also alter the GK's approach to their positioning.

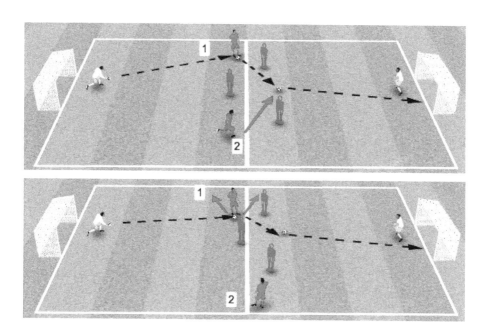

Progressions:

If there are additional players, rotate them into the practice.

Change how, and where, the GK starts each repetition from.

Allow attacking players to go 'all in' so they have no restrictions and play what they see.

GK Learning Detail:

Technical: Technical response based upon the finishing range (1v1, short or longer-range strike) | Ability to manoeuvre the ball away from immediate danger (hand shapes based upon the pace of the ball)

Tactical: Initial start position when the opposite GK has the ball – the length of the practice will be a big factor on this | Movement and positioning if wide attacker touches the ball to shoot

Psychological: Speed of assessment off the attacking players first touch and their direction of movement | If the ball is played across (diagram 2) can the GK cut out the ball? This will start first time, so the attacking player can work on a first-time finish but progress to any touches which will bring an air of unpredictability | Don't guess or pre-empt too early what the attacking players will do – maintain a pro-active mindset to anticipate events (it's a fine balance between anticipation and guesswork)

Physical: Ability to move with speed and control to defend the area initially from the combination play | Set position and balance upon the attacker's strike on goal | General speed and agility to change position quickly to respond to the movement of the ball | Ability to show an appropriate body position if engaging the ball for a 1v1 save

Social/Environmental: If there are two GKs working, build-in some challenges e.g. point scoring system | Pair a GK up with one attacker to act as a team together – first to five goals, for example| Focus on consistency of actions and appropriateness of decision making

Outfield Learning Detail:

Technical: The weight and accuracy of passing, combination play, and through balls | Consistency and detail of technical proficiency | Encourage different types of finishes | Ensure their first touch (or any ball manipulation) keeps them within the width of the goal if possible

Tactical: Assess the GKs' positions in the goals as this can dictate the attackers' decision on how to strike the ball | Look to play away from mannequins to create new space and angles to finish

Psychological: Confidence to try new techniques | Quick decisions on what to do with the ball – have a plan and be pro-active

Physical: Snap shots with no backlift – as the GK may be caught moving or off-guard | Speed of movement and front foot mentality | General balance and co-ordination to strike the ball first time or whilst body is in motion

Social/Environmental: Place emphasis on the attacking players playing at match tempo/intensity and being ruthless in front of goal – trying to score at every attempt; this applies to any rebounds off the GKs as well.

78

Goalkeeping Themes: General shot stopping from different distances and angles.

Practice Objectives: To give GKs repeated exposure to shot stopping scenarios in a fluid environment. For the attacking players, it's a chance to work on different types of finishing – both with the ball and moving onto a passed ball.

Description: The ball will start from a wide server (player or coach). They can play into either of the two attacking players who attack the goal closest to them. These attackers will make movements around the playing area before receiving the ball to attack their goal. Examples of some constraints that have been used. A) Attacker has one touch then shoots. B) Attacker has a time limit. C) Attacker has a touch limit. The two diagrams show that the practice can be altered in terms of the distance between the central start point and the goal.

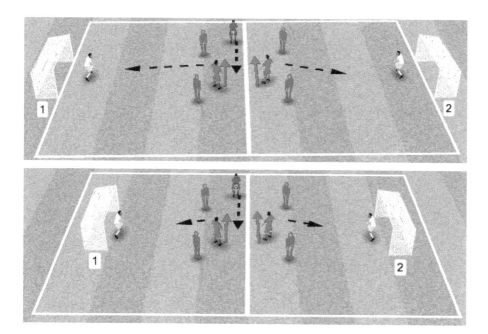

Progressions:

The receiving attacker travels to the goal furthest away from them.

As above, but the other attacking player acts a defender and, if they win the ball, they can attack the opposite goal.

GK Learning Detail:

Technical: Technical response based upon the finishing range (1v1, short or longer-range strike) | Ability to manoeuvre the ball away from immediate danger (hand shapes based upon the pace of the ball)

Tactical: Initial start position when server/coach has the ball – the length of the practice is a big factor on this | Movement and positioning if wide attacker touches the ball to shoot | Make sure the GK is set before the initial contact from the attacker in case they decide to shoot first time

Psychological: Speed of assessment off the attacking players' first touch and their direction of movement | Don't guess or pre-empt too early what the attacking players will do; maintain a pro-active mindset to anticipate (it's a fine balance between anticipation and guesswork)

Physical: Ability to move with speed and control to defend the area initially from the combination play | Set position and balance upon the attacker's strike on goal | General speed and agility to change position quickly to respond to the movement of the ball | Ability to show an appropriate body position if engaging the ball for a 1v1 save

Social/Environmental: Pair a GK up with one attacker to act as a team together – first to five goals, for example| Focus on consistency of actions and appropriateness of decision making

Outfield Learning Detail:

Technical: The weight and accuracy of passing, combination play, and through balls | Consistency and detail of GKs' technical proficiency | Encourage different types of finishing | Ensure their first touch (or any ball manipulation) keeps them within the width of the goal if possible

Tactical: Assess the GKs' positions in the goals as this can dictate the attackers' decision on how to strike the ball | Look to play away from mannequins to create new space and angles to finish

Psychological: Confidence to try new techniques | Quick decisions on what to do with the ball – have a plan and be pro-active

Physical: Snap shots with no backlift – as the GK may be caught moving or off-guard | Speed of movement and front foot mentality | General balance and co-ordination to strike the ball first time or whilst body is in motion

Social/Environmental: Place emphasis on the attacking players playing at match tempo/intensity and being ruthless in front of goal – trying to score at every attempt; this applies to any rebounds off the GKs as well.

79

Goalkeeping Themes: Reaction saves and protecting the goal from first time finishes – 1-6 yards.

Practice Objectives: To provide the GKs with an environment that is geared around fast-paced finishing in order to develop quick thinking and application. For attacking players, the emphasis will be on adapting their body shape to finish first time (including volleys, half volleys, and heading)

Description: The ball starts from either ball position 1, 2, or 3 – if there are more than two players available then the practice can start from two or three entry points at a time. The ball is played in at any pace, height, or trajectory into the attacking player and they can score in any of the three goals, but this must be a first-time finish. The attacker can position and move anywhere in the playing zone. The distance of the server away from the goals can vary along with the size of goals – depending on the age and/or ability of the GKs who are working. Any balls that are left in the playing area can be rebounded into any goal, first time, by the attacking player.

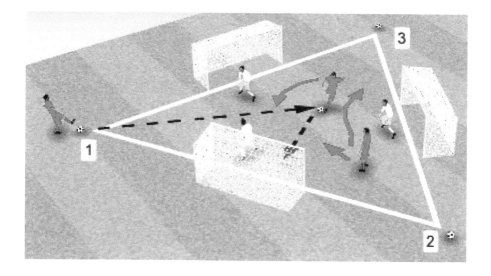

Progressions:

Rotate the GKs into different goals.

Change the size of each goal (if possible).

The entry point server can also shoot at any goal.

GK Learning Detail:

Technical: Head position is crucial and will dictate each GK's stance and ability keep their shape | Observe when to use leg saves | Look to repel and deflect the ball away (rather than letting the ball hit the keeper directly) | Determine which body part to use in order to be effective and do not be afraid to be 'unorthodox'

Tactical: As the ball is played in, move towards the half of the goal where the initial contact will take place | From the ball that's played in, can the GK cut this out? Or can they close down the ball to make a block save before the initial contact?

Psychological: It's the GK vs the ball! | Desire to keep the ball out the net |To carry on giving 100% effort and focus in the face of adversity | Bravery to be hit on the body from a short-range | Speed of decision making in terms of how to best keep the ball out of the goal

Physical: Speed and co-ordination of body and limbs | Footwork patterns to re-adjust to the type of delivery from the wide server, and to be in control of this movement pattern

Social/Environmental: The practice is designed to really test the GKs in terms of the level of success they will enjoy – make sure they understand that there will be goals and that any save from this range can be classified as success! | Have a competition to see who concedes the fewest goals

Outfield Learning Detail:

Technical: The initial passing detail from the wide server (based upon how they've decided the ball will be played to the attacking player) |How the attacker adapts and/or re-adjusts to the flight of the ball | Does their technical response give them the best chance of scoring – pace vs placement of the ball

Tactical: Observation of where the GK is, from the attacker's initial contact

Psychological: Decide upon the technique and which goal the attacker wants to go to | Confidence to keep finishing despite maybe missing chances

Physical: Agility, balance, and co-ordination of movement from the attacker and effectiveness of the technical finish

Social/Environmental: Place emphasis on the attacking players playing at match tempo/intensity and being ruthless in front of goal – trying to score at every attempt; this applies to any rebounds off the GKs as well

80

Goalkeeping Themes: Defending the goal against quick combination play and cutbacks.

Practice Objectives: To provide GKs with an environment where they are exposed to ball movement and lateral passes across the face of their goals. For the attackers, this is a chance to work on quick shifts of play and finishing from different angles, and with differing numbers of touches.

Description: The ball starts in a wide position with both of the wide outfield players. Either of these players can pass the ball into a grid (size can vary) for attacker 1 or 2 to receive the ball with the two attackers being allowed to move around the grid. Depending on the weight of pass, these attacking players can shoot first time or off a first touch at either goal. Both attackers can rebound off the first shot on goal. The practice will be reset after each repetition. There are a few progressions to this practice which are stated below.

Progressions:

Once attacker 1 or 2 receives the ball, they can lay the ball back for a wide player to shoot first time at either goal – with both attacking players rebounding.

The receiving attacking player can combine with the other attacking player to try and score.

Bring in a touch or time limit to the practice to maintain realism and intensity.

Rotate the attacking players' roles and positions and alter the grid size.

GK Learning Detail:

Technical: Technical response based upon the finishing range (1v1, short or longer-range strike) | Ability to manoeuvre the ball away from immediate danger (hand shapes based upon the pace of the ball)

Tactical: Initial positioning from the wide ball and following the path of the ball – don't stand still for too long

Psychological: Speed of assessment off the attacking player's first touch and their direction of movement | Being able to respond quickly to performance cues, e.g. loose ball, attacker in control of ball, the ball going backwards, and the trigger for the attacker to shoot | Don't guess or pre-empt too early what the attacking players will do; maintain a pro-active mindset to anticipate events (there's a fine balance between anticipation and guesswork)

Physical: Ability to move with speed and control to defend the area from the initial combination play | Set position and balance upon the attacker's strike on goal | General speed and agility to change position quickly to respond to the movement of the ball | Ability to show an appropriate body position if engaging the ball for a 1v1 save

Social/Environmental: Focus on consistency of actions and appropriateness of decision making | A competition between both GK and also the attacking players

Outfield Learning Detail:

Technical: The weight and accuracy of passing, combination play, and through balls | Consistency and detail of players' technical proficiency | Encourage different types of finish | Ensure first touches (or any manipulation) keeps them closer within the width of the goal

Tactical: Assess the GKs position in the goal as this can dictate an attacker's decision on how to strike the ball | Look to play away from mannequins to create new space and angles to finish

Psychological: Confidence to try new techniques | Quick decisions on what to do with the ball – have a plan and be pro-active and communicate with teammates

Physical: Snap shots with no backlift – as the GK may be caught moving or off-guard | Speed of movement and front foot mentality | General balance and co-ordination to strike the ball first time or whilst body is in motion

Social/Environmental: Place emphasis on the attacking players playing at match tempo/intensity and being ruthless in front of goal – trying to score at every attempt; this applies to any rebounds off the GKs as well.

81

Goalkeeping Themes: Central shot stopping and defending the goal from volleys.

Practice Objectives: To give the GK practice in defending the goal against loose balls, first time snap finishes, and also different types of volley. For the attacking players, this practice develops volleying techniques, and has players judging passes and striking the ball first time.

Description: The ball starts centrally on the floor from the attacker. They pass the ball into a server who then plays the ball back at any height but at a pace that allows the attacker to shoot first time. The server's distance away from the attacker can vary (to mix up the pass back) and also the distance between the two goals can be altered depending on the shooting range the GKs are working on. With there being two goals, the attacker can rotate the goal they are striking at.

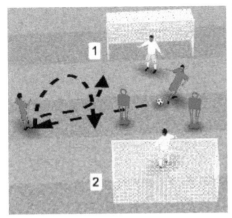 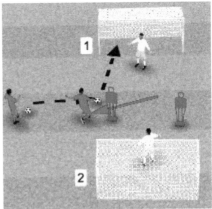

Progressions:

The attacking player can shoot in either goal.

Change the side of the serving player.

Two attacking players shooting on goal (rotate every number of attempts or every goal).

GK Learning Detail:

Technical: Head position is crucial and will dictate the GK's stance and ability keep their shape | Observe when to use leg saves | Look to repel and deflect the ball away rather than letting the ball hit the GK | Which body part to use in order to be effective and not afraid to be 'unorthodox' | From volleys, pick up the flight and trajectory of the ball which will bring in top hand saves

Tactical: If the ball coming back from the server is bouncing, don't advance | Speed to adapt positioning based upon the travelling ball

Psychological: It's the GK vs the ball! | Desire to keep the ball out the net | To carry on giving 100% effort and focus in the face of adversity | Bravery to be hit on the body from a short-range distance | Speed of decision making in terms of how best to keep the ball out of the goal

Physical: Speed and co-ordination of body and limbs | Footwork patterns to re-adjust to the type of delivery from the wide server, and to be in control of this movement pattern | Potentially backwards movements from volleys – observe this movement, plus an emphasis dropping the shoulder rather than purely back-peddling

Social/Environmental: The practice is designed to really test the GKs in terms of how much success they will enjoy; make sure they understand that there will be goals and that any save from this range can be classified as success! | Have a competition to see who concedes the fewest goals

Outfield Learning Detail:

Technical: The initial passing detail from the wide server (based upon how they've decided the ball will be played to the attacking player) | How the attacker adapts and/or re-adjusts to the flight of the ball | Does their technical response give them the best chance of scoring – pace vs placement of the ball | Full volley and half volley technique – focus on the point of contact on the ball

Tactical: Observation of where the GK is from the attacker's initial contact

Psychological: Decide upon the technique and which goal the attacker wants to go to | Confidence to keep finishing despite maybe missing chances

Physical: Agility, balance, and co-ordination of movements from the attacker, and the effectiveness of the technical finish

Social/Environmental: Place emphasis on the attacking players playing at match tempo/intensity and being ruthless in front of goal – trying to score at every attempt; this applies to any rebounds off the GKs as well

82

Goalkeeping Themes: Cut back situations – incorporating potential 1v1s.

Practice Objectives: To allow the GK to work on their assessment, movement, positioning, and save execution from cut back situations and wide areas. For the defender(s) to practice defending the area. For the attacking players, this exercise develops their movement timing, crossing detail, and first-time finishing.

Description: The ball starts with attacker 1. They have the option to either go 1v1 with the defender, or try to score, or they can play to wide attackers 2 or 3. Once the ball goes wide, 2 and 3 can travel past the mannequin and play a crossed ball to attacker 1 (who runs into the box) and to the opposite attacker (who will come in to the back post). If the defender wins the ball, they will have a target zone outside the play area, which the GK will also use if they secure the ball.

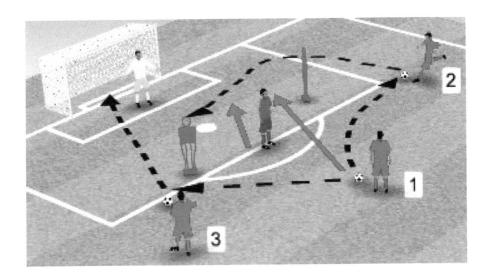

Progressions:

Attackers 2 and 3 can cut inside and shoot.

All three attackers rotate sides to work on left and right foot deliveries.

GK Learning Detail:

Technical: Head position is crucial and will dictate the GK's stance and ability keep their shape | Observe when to use leg saves | Look to repel and deflect the ball away rather than letting the ball hit themselves | Which body part to use in order to be effective and not afraid to be 'unorthodox' | From volleys or headers, pick up the flight and trajectory of the ball which will bring in top hand saves

Tactical: Positioning from the crossed ball – don't overcompensate at the front post | Assess whether it is a left or right footed cross | Information to the defender to aid their defensive duties

Psychological: Assessment of the flight and trajectory of the cross – can they affect the ball | If not coming for the ball, then look at the GK's recovery position and make sure they don't look to track the ball but turn their head to the anticipated point of contact from the attackers

Physical: Efficiency and control of movement laterally and vertically around the goalmouth | Speed of upper limbs and lower limbs | Observe the GK's head position upon contact – is it close to the ball? Ability to generate power from a standing stance

Social/Environmental: The practice is designed to really test the GKs in terms of the level of success they can achieve – make sure they understand that there will be goals and that any save from this range can be classified as success! | Have a competition to see who concedes the fewest number of goals

Outfield Learning Detail:

Technical: The pass and cross detail from all attacking players | Technical proficiency of the first-time finish with a focus on the attacking player's point of contact | Clearances from the defender – is this with the correct body part and is this with height and distance

Tactical: Defender(s) protection of the goal and body shape/intention to do so | Attacking movement based upon the picture in front of them (defender's positioning and the direction of the cross) | Finishing type – is this appropriate based upon the position the attacker finds themselves in

Psychological: Concentration throughout the whole practice | Is the cross of appropriate detail (pace, height, and direction of the ball) for the attacker's positioning and the timing/movement of their runs

Physical: Movement timing and adjustment in accordance with the ball | Attacking players ability to create space away from the defender | Co-ordination and striking balance when crossing and finishing first time

Social/Environmental: Place emphasis on the attacking players playing at match tempo/intensity and being ruthless in front of goal – trying to score at every attempt; this applies to any rebounds off the GKs as well

83

Goalkeeping Themes: Small-sided Game – GK initiating the attack.

Practice Objectives: To allow the GK to be a focal point for the team's attacking strategy by starting with the ball at every opportunity. This can be used for a section of a team-based session. Here they can work on various kinds of distribution to different thirds of the pitches. The practice also helps the team to work on different shapes for the GK to play out to, and for the individuals involved to trust and understand the importance of the GK being a focal point.

Description: A normal small-sided game (7v7 or 8v8, etc.). The main thing that promotes the use of the GK as a playmaker is that every time the ball leaves the field of play, either one of the GKs can start the practice (the team that lost the ball relinquishes possession or the coach can dictate who starts). The ball can start from the GK either with them getting a ball positioned by the goal or a coach/server playing the ball to a GK from a central position. Other rules and factors can, of course, be implemented depending on the team's session.

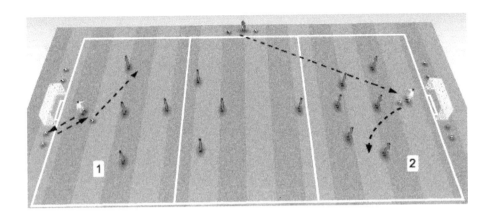

Progressions:

Bring the above GK rule (that they start with the ball) in and out of the session at different points – to incorporate the GK into the team-based session.

Change the pitch's dimensions to emphasise shorter-range distribution and playing under greater pressure.

GK Learning Detail:

Technical: Playability of passes | Technical range (age/ability dependant)

Tactical: GKs' support positions (based on how you want them to play) | Seeing the situation in front of them and being a thinker of the game – 'what do I need to do in this specific situation?' | Appropriateness of distribution based on the situation in front of them

Psychological: Ability to stay composed and in control under pressure | Be pro-active and have a plan before the ball is received | Speed of assessment of the picture in front of them and the consistency of their distribution

Physical: Speed and control of body to move into different support positions | Balance and consistency of first touch | Ability to manipulate the ball with both feet and play off different numbers of touches

Social/Environmental: Do the GKs show a desire to have the ball and does their body language reflect this

Outfield Learning Detail:

Individual's movement and body shape to receive the ball.

Willingness to get on the ball and to trust the GK to use them in open play as well.

Potential rotation of players to create space to play.

Don't delay if a player is going to play to the GK as the more time taken, the more pressure they're likely to be under.

84

Goalkeeping Themes: Small-sided game – GK initiating the attack with a focus on wide areas.

Practice Objectives: To allow the GK to be a focal point of the team's attacking strategy by starting with the ball at every opportunity. This can be used for a section of a team-based session. Here they can work on various kinds of distribution to different thirds of the pitches. Also, of value for the team to work on different shapes for the GK to play out to, and for the individuals involved to trust and understand the importance of the GK being a focal point.

Description: A normal small-sided game (7v7 or 8v8, etc.). The main thing that promotes the use of the GK as a playmaker is that every time the ball leaves the field of play, either one of the GKs can start the practice (the team that lost the ball relinquishes possession or the coach can dictate who starts). The ball can start from the GK, with them getting a ball positioned by the goal, or from a coach/server playing the ball to a GK from a central position. The main change to the previous practice is that the wide areas (at first) are unopposed zones to allow the GKs to work on their wide distribution range and accuracy in order to build confidence and familiarity. Other rules and factors can, of course, be utilised, depending on the team's session.

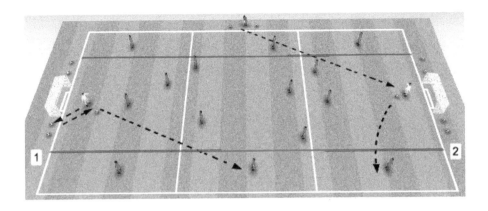

Progressions:

Bring the above GK rule (that they start with the ball) in and out of the session at different points – to incorporate the GK into the team-based session.

Change the pitch's dimensions to emphasise shorter-range distribution and playing under more pressure.

GK Learning Detail:

Technical: Playability of passes | Technical range (age/ability dependant)

Tactical: GKs' support position (based upon how you want them to play) | Seeing the situation in front of them and being a thinker of the game – 'what do I need to do in this specific situation?' | Appropriateness of distribution based on the situation in front of them

Psychological: Ability to stay composed and in control under pressure | Be pro-active and have a plan before the ball is received | Speed of assessment of the picture in front of them, and the consistency of their distribution

Physical: Speed and control of body to move into different support positions | Balance and consistency of first touch | Ability to manipulate the ball with both feet and play off different numbers of touches

Social/Environmental: Do the GKs show a desire to have the ball and does their body language reflect this?

Outfield Learning Detail:

Individual's movement and body shape to receive the ball.

Willingness to get on the ball and to trust the GK to use it in open play as well.

Potential rotation of players to create space to play.

Don't delay if a player is going to play to the GK; the more time taken, the more pressure they're likely to be under.

85

Goalkeeping Themes: Shot stopping scenarios within the penalty area.

Practice Objectives: To give the GK an environment of fast-moving balls, blocked vision, and the need to assess different types of shot on goal. In turn, second phase recovery saves, and when/how to defend the goal, are offered. For attacking players, this practice works on getting shots away quickly and analysing when space opens up. Defenders will work on emergency defending (blocks, interceptions, and putting their bodies on the line).

Description: There are four (or any number available) servers located outside the penalty area, each with a ball; they can either be stationary or freely moving. Upon a call from the coach, or server, a numbered player plays the ball into the penalty area where a 2v2 will occur with the attacking team trying to score and the defending team trying to block/intercept, etc. If the defender wins the ball, they can play to an outside server or add in a clearance target zone away from the playing area (the GK is included in this). The ball is always in play until either in the goal or outside the penalty area.

Progressions:

Rotate positions in the practice.

The serving players can shoot and/or be rebound players for the attacking team.

Build in a competition and have players in teams.

Decrease the number of defenders or add attackers (2v3) or vice versa to overload the defence (3v2).

GK Learning Detail:

Technical: Technical response to the attempt on goal | Identify when and where to use top or bottom hand, and also leg saves

Tactical: Positioning – observation in relation to the ball but also the defending players | Ability to manoeuvre the ball out of the penalty area – wrist and hand strength

Psychological: Information/communication to defenders – content, tone of voice, appropriateness of information | Ability to assess and execute technical response with maximum speed

Physical: Footwork to cover the goal laterally | Diving and jumping actions from a standing stance | Set position and stance at point of contact | Don't be afraid to produce 'unorthodox' movement patterns away from more traditional lines of thinking

Social/Environmental: Desire to defend the goal from ALL situations – even ones where there seems no hope in saving the ball

Outfield Learning Detail:

Technical: Defenders' ability to stay big and block shots (head and hips square onto the ball) | Initial pass from the serving players and their detail of passes if involved as a rebounder | Attackers' shooting range and decision making based upon the picture they see

Tactical: All outfield players' ability to adapt to the picture they see once the ball has been played in from a server

Psychological: Defenders' decisions on how, where, and when to press the ball and their timing to engage/win it | Do the attackers assess the defenders' and GK's position early, to best inform how they approach that individual repetition within the practice as each attack will be different

Physical: Defenders' ability to decelerate and show away from goal | Can the attacker adjust their body to receive and shoot in one movement | Overall balance and control of body when passing, moving, and striking on goal

Social/Environmental: Ruthlessness of the attackers to score, and of the defenders not to concede!

86

Goalkeeping Themes: General handling and movement patterns.

Practice Objectives: To give the GKs lots of handling situations and put them in positions where they need to assess the flight, trajectory, pace, and general pathway of the ball. Outfield players will work on passing range, first touch, and moving the ball quickly.

Description: Based upon the first diagram below – there are two balls with two GKs working in the middle of a circular grid – 10x10 yards in diameter. The GKs have to stop the ball reaching another outfield player whilst the ball goes through the grid. The outfielder players have to miss a player out when the ball goes through the grid (they can't play to the person next to them). The players can be stationary or moving. If the GK claims the ball, they play to a player without a ball. Height constraints can be built into the practice. Emphasise the need for all passes to not only beat the GK but be controlled by the receiving player so they can then play a pass.

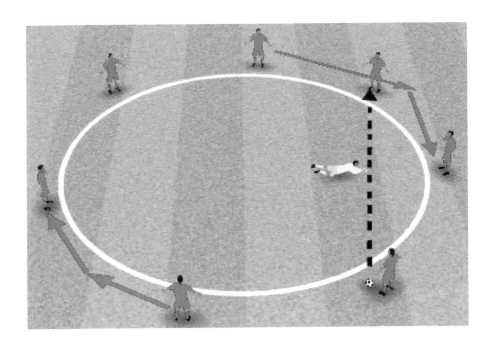

Progressions:

Change the size of the playing grid – and also the shape.

Apply a height constraint to avoid loopy balls over the GK which they will never reach.

Put time or touch constraints on the outfield players.

Have one GK working at a time.

Make the practice time limited – so the GK(s) aren't working aerobically for a prolonged period of time.

GK Learning Detail:

Technical: General specific handling and footwork objectives for the GKs who are working – hand shapes, movement fluency, and consistency

Tactical: No real tactical detail within this practice

Psychological: Ability to assess the ball's movement and show a willingness to treat every ball with 100% focus

Physical: Speed and fluency of movement patterns | Control and balance of body | Agility and flexibility to cover different distances depending on the passing patterns of the outfield players

Social/Environmental: Treat every ball as an opportunity to work on handling and movement patterns | If two GKs are working, build a mini competition into the practice

Outfield Learning Detail:

Quality of first touch to control.

Communication on when to set the ball, and who the ball is being played to.

Detail on passes – weight, accuracy, and playability.

Assessment on where the GK(s) is positioned and looking for space to play passes into

87

Goalkeeping Themes: Reaction saves and loose ball assessment.

Practice Objectives: To create situations for the GKs where there is a loose ball within close-range proximity to the goal. Attackers will work on first time attempts on goal from different angles.

Description: A server starts with the ball from a central position. They play a randomly weighted and directed ball into the penalty area for attacker 1 or 2 to finish in any goal, first time. If any of the three GKs save the ball back into the penalty area, either attacker can shoot first time into any of the three goals. Practice starts again once the ball is out of play or a score has been made. If any of the GKs secure the ball, they will play back to the central serving player.

Progressions:

Change the position of the central server.

Change the pass delivery detail from the central server – can be in the air or bouncing, etc.

If a GK secures the ball, they can distribute/try and score in either of the other two goals.

Make the playing area smaller for closer-range saves or larger for longer-range situations.

GK Learning Detail:

Technical: Technical response based upon the situation – 1v1 save or a shot-stopping technique | Assess the position of the ball being struck early, to get angles and distances right

Tactical: Assessment of whether to leave the goal (can the GK cover the space) or whether to stay in a deeper position to defend the goal | Stay alert and in a position to affect the ball (or defend the goal) after an initial attempt on goal

Psychological: Observe the GKs' focus and concentration during each repetition and their ability to respond to environmental cues and triggers – such as loose balls, danger situations, or impending attempts on goal | Desire and mentality to keep the ball out the goal and to be realistic with some of the attempts they make – keep a positive mindset

Physical: Key observation on the GKs' set positions upon any strike on goal | When the GK is in motion, observe if the distance they need to cover requires arm movement; longer distances will need arm movement to travel | Speed to cover space to engage the ball for 1v1 situations | Control of body to decelerate and/or adjust to the movement of the ball

Social/Environmental: Use the practice as a chance to develop a ruthless mentality to defend the goal! | Encourage individuality from the GKs in order to defend the goal

Outfield Learning Detail:

Attackers' ability to adjust their body to finish first time from every pass into the area.

Attackers' assessment of the GK(s)' movement and positioning.

Attackers' awareness of rebound situations.

88

Goalkeeping Themes: Cut back situations and lateral movement across the goal area.

Practice Objectives: To give the GK practice on assessing cut back situations – in terms of positioning, decision making, and their technical responses. Attacking players will work on close-range finishing, the timing of movements, and the detail of their passes.

Description: The ball starts with player 1 who travels past a mannequin (or equivalent piece of equipment) into a wide area. They will play the ball across the face of the goal for player 2, who then attempts to score – make sure this player is not offside. If the GK secures the ball, they distribute to player 3. Player 3 will also have a ball and can attempt a second shot on goal if the situation is appropriate and allows progression – e.g. the ball is deflected back out, down the centre of the pitch.

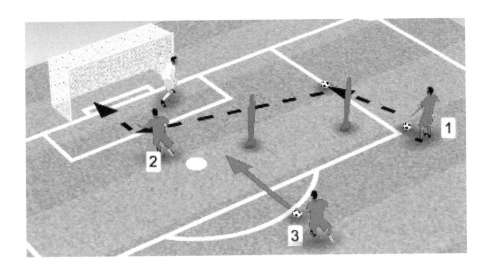

Progressions:

Rotate sides and roles.

The practice can start from player 3 who passes to player 1 who then begins their movement.

Encourage player 1 to travel towards the goal as well as towards the by-line.

GK Learning Detail:

Technical: Technical responses that prevent rebounds on goal from either attacking player | How the GK keeps the ball out from player 2 – be adaptable and focus on saving the ball not necessary how you do it (observe head position with this detail)

Tactical: Ability to cover the necessary space if the ball is squared to attacker 2, based upon their position and the pathway of the ball | GK's position in relation to the post – don't overcompensate and come outside the line of the post

Psychological: Assessment of attacker 1's first touch and how this impacts their decision of how and where to move | Allow the GK to try different techniques so they build up the confidence to develop their own style to defend the goal | Does the GK give up on possible lost causes, or do they throw their body on the line

Physical: Key observation on the GK's set position upon strike on goal | When the GK is in motion, observe if the distance they need to cover requires arm movement – longer distances will require arm movements to travel | Work on the crossover step to cover more distance

Social/Environmental: Use the practice as a chance to develop a ruthless mentality to defend the goal!

Outfield Learning Detail:

Technical: Overall finishing and ball striking technique | Adaptability to assess the picture and respond technically in a consistent manner

Tactical: Observation of the GK's positioning and how best to score based on the visual information available

Psychological: Early assessment of different type of finish to use | Attacker's ability to move into an early position to strike – depending on the flight and trajectory of the ball

Physical: Balance upon receiving touches and ball striking | Stability of striking technique and foot manipulation of the ball (side foot, laces, curling, etc.)

Social/Environmental: Being clinical in front of goal and enjoying scoring – also from any rebounds from the GK | Make sure the attackers finish the repetition with a goal when possible

89

Goalkeeping Themes: Quick fire shooting and reaction save situations.

Practice Objectives: To expose the GK to a fast-paced, high-tempo, and competitive environment where they can work on all facets of reaction saves such as speed, agility, and ball assessment. For outfield players, the 2v2 will provide the opportunity to work on emergency defending, creating and scoring, and all-round shooting ruthlessness – clinical finishing at every opportunity.

Description: Within the penalty area, there are three teams of two players whose objective is to work together to try and score. The ball starts outside the area in a 5x10-yard grid. The serving player can play the ball anywhere into the penalty area with all the players moving freely. If a goal is scored, the ball starts with the serving player; if the GK secures the ball, they distribute it back to the serving player also. The ball is always in play unless it goes out of the penalty area. If the ball is won by a team, they can go straight in and score.

Progressions:

The ball can start from the GK as well.

If the GK secures the ball, they can play the ball back out into the penalty area.

Work on different entries from the serving player (direction, distance, angles, and pace/height of pass into the penalty area).

GK Learning Detail:

Technical: Ability to use all body parts to save the ball; there will be attempts from different ranges, with bodies in the way, and because of the competition there will be unpredictability

Tactical: Recovery saves – because of the nature of the practice, the likelihood of being able to deflect the ball away from players, at all times, is low – hence the second save, or ability of the GK to return to feet, is crucial

Psychological: Observe the GK's focus and concentration during each repetition and their ability to respond to environmental cues and triggers such as loose balls, danger situations, or impending attempts on goal | Desire and mentality to keep the ball out the goal and to be realistic with the attempts they can make – keep a positive mindset

Physical: Footwork to cover the goal laterally | Diving and jumping actions from a standing stance | Set position and stance at point of contact | Don't be afraid to produce 'unorthodox' movement patterns away from more traditional lines of thinking

Social/Environmental: Embrace the chaos!

Outfield Learning Detail:

Desire to get on the ball, but also to win the ball back from the opposition team.

Defenders' posture and distance while closing down.

Defenders' ability to decelerate and force the attackers away from goal.

Defenders' timing of interceptions; the second defender's cover and balance.

Defenders' desire to block shots.

Attackers' decision making – have a plan.

Attackers' ability to identify when the space opens up to shoot.

Attackers' ruthlessness in front goal.

Attackers' creativity and unpredictability on, and away from, the ball.

90

Goalkeeping Themes: Distribution methods incorporating shot stopping from 14+ yards.

Practice Objectives: To provide the GK with a platform to practise different types of distribution whilst building on some key shot stopping principles and situations. For the attacking players, this is a chance to work on their first touches and their ability to shift/manoeuvre the ball into a shooting opportunity quickly.

Description: The GK starts with the ball and plays it to player 1 – this can be through any method but a good place to start is a clip or drive into the player. Player 1 is then allowed maximum of two touches before shooting or squaring the ball to player 2 for a strike on goal. Rebounds are in play during the practice. The practice then begins again.

Progressions:

No touch limit on players.

Change the positioning of the receiving player and player 2.

Work both sides of the pitch.

The GK can use any type of distribution.

GK Learning Detail:

Technical: Distribution detail – is the ball controllable but then playable for the attacker off the next touch | Technical response that won't allow rebounds on goal from either attacking player

Tactical: With the focus on longer-range shooting – observe the GK's depth and lateral position | Ability to cover the necessary space if the ball is squared to attacker 2 based upon their position and the pathway of the ball

Psychological: Assessment of attacker 1's first touch and how this impacts upon their decision of how and where to move | Allow the GK to try different techniques so they build up the confidence to develop their own style to defend the goal

Physical: Key observation on the GK's set position upon any strike on goal | When the GK is in motion, observe if the distance they need to cover requires arm movement; longer distances will need arm movement to travel | Work on the crossover step to cover more distance

Social/Environmental: Use the practice as a chance to develop a ruthless mentality to defend the goal!

Outfield Learning Detail:

Technical: Overall finishing and ball striking technique | Adaptability to assess the picture and respond technically in a consistent manner

Tactical: Observation of the GK's positioning and how best to score based on the visual information available to them

Psychological: Early assessment of different types of finish to use | Attacker's ability to move into an early position to strike – depending on the flight and trajectory of the ball

Physical: Balance upon receiving touches and ball striking | Stability of striking technique and foot manipulation of the ball (side foot, laces, curling, etc.)

Social/Environmental: Being clinical in front of goal and enjoying scoring – also from any rebounds from the GK | Make sure the attackers finish the repetition with a goal when possible

91

Goalkeeping Themes: Distribution methods and defending the area/defending the goal.

Practice Objectives: To allow the GK to work on various types of passes, volleys, and throws, along with being exposed to a 2v2 situation where they defend the area initially before defending the goal based upon the situation in front of them. For defending players, this practice will develop their pressure timing and techniques, their blocking, and also intercepting. For the attacking players, it's a chance to work on their combination play, how they create chances, and (ultimately) their goal scoring.

Description: The GK starts with the ball and plays to either of the two attacking players (A). As soon as the ball is released, two defenders (D) engage the attackers and try to deny them scoring. The 2v2 is in play for as long as the ball is in the area, but a time limit of five seconds can be put on the attackers to encourage fast attacking. If the GK secures the ball, they hold on to it and the practice is reset. If the defenders win the ball, they look to retain possession and play to waiting attacking players or into a target zone/goal. The players defending and attacking will rotate after every repetition.

Progressions:

Change any constraints on the attacking players.

Start the attacking players closer or further away from goal, or even wider/more central.

Make the practice competitive with both teams performing both roles and keeping score; whichever team scores the most in a certain number of repetitions or time frame is the winner.

GK Learning Detail:

Technical: Response to the particular attempt on goal with a focus on their ability to deflect/manoeuvre the ball away from the playing area | Assessment on what range the attempt on goal is from, and how best to deal with this particular ball

Tactical: Initial starting position after the attacker has made initial contact on the ball | Decision on whether to defend the space by cutting out a loose ball or to engage the attacker

Psychological: Make the ball the priority! | Assessment on how far to change position laterally – not going too tight on the post if the keeper needs to cover the space from a ball across the face of goal | Confidence to leave the goal if necessary and adopt positive body language

Physical: Ability to make close-range reaction saves involving fast limb movement | Head position on diving and jumping movements | Balance and body composure when changing position, based upon the picture in front on them

Social/Environmental: Information and communication to the defenders | Being dominant and in control of the situation | If there are two GKs then a mini competition can be created to test motivation

Outfield Learning Detail:

Defenders' posture and distance while closing down.

Defenders' ability to decelerate and force the attackers away from goal.

Defenders' timing of interceptions; second defender's cover and balance.

Defenders' desire to block shots.

Attackers' decision making – have a plan.

Attackers' ability to identify when the space opens up to shoot.

Attackers' ruthlessness in front goal.

Attackers' creativity and unpredictability on and away from the ball.

92

Goalkeeping Themes: Starting attacks in a small-sided possession practice.

Practice Objectives: To allow the GK to start and build attacks, while working on different types of distribution, and into different areas of the pitch. For the team, in general, this exercise will work on patterns when the GK has the ball in their possession – both in play and from different start positions.

Description: A standard small-sided directional practice (6v6 shown on a 40x60-yard pitch, but this can change of course) sets the scene. The ball will always start from the GK if the ball goes off the pitch – this can be from a server playing the ball from a central position, as shown, or directly from the GK who has extra balls positioned near the goal. Both teams are trying to build attacks to get the ball to the opposite GK. If they're successful, they get a point and the ball will start from their GK or from the central server. The practice will continue until a pre-determined number of points are scored or a particular time period has elapsed.

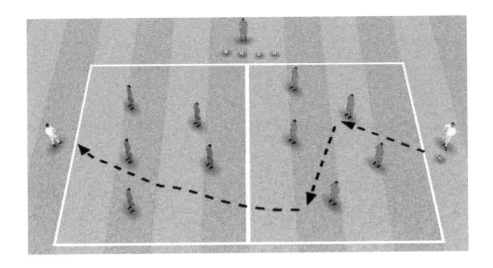

Progressions:

If a team reaches the opposite GK, the ball starts with the other team.

The GK can play directly to the opposite GK if they see the opportunity to do so.

Overload one team to change the difficulty for both teams.

Add in different rules to change the challenge for the GK – e.g. don't allow them to be pressed, in order to build confidence.

Change the pitch dimensions – e.g. shorter pitch to give the GK less time and more immediate pressure.

GK Learning Detail:

Technical: Playability of passes | Technical range (age/ability dependant)

Tactical: GKs' support positions (based upon how you want them to play) | Seeing the situation in front of them and being a thinker of the game – 'what do I need to do in this specific situation?' | Distribution appropriateness based on the situation in front of them

Psychological: Ability to stay composed and in control under pressure | Being pro-active and having a plan before the ball is received | Speed of assessment of the picture in front of them | Consistency of distribution

Physical: Speed and control of body to move into different support positions | Balance and consistency of first touch | Ability to manipulate the ball with both feet and play off different numbers of touches

Social/Environmental: Do the GKs show a desire to have the ball and does their body language reflect this?

Outfield Learning Detail:

Each individual's movement and body shape to receive the ball.

Willingness to get on the ball and to trust the GK to use them in open play as well.

Potential rotation of players to create space to play.

Don't delay if a player is going to play to the GK as, the more time taken, the more pressure they're likely to be under.

93

Goalkeeping Themes: Shot stopping scenarios with a focus on communication/information.

Practice Objectives: To expose the GK to different types of shot stopping scenarios whilst having a main objective of limiting attempts on goal through effective organisation and giving the right information (at the right time) to defenders. For the defenders, this exercise works on emergency defending and preventing through balls, combination plays, and attempts on goal. For the attacking players, work focuses on unlocking a defensive block in front of the goal.

Description: There are two small-sided games happening at the same time with the balls starting in the middle of the pitch. The games are 3v3, as shown, in the diagrams with the pitch being 20x30 yards (both can be adapted). An attacking player will retrieve a ball from the middle and look to attack the goal and score. The ball is in play until that repetition has come to a conclusion. If the defenders win the ball, they will look to keep the ball for five passes or play to pre-determined target zones.

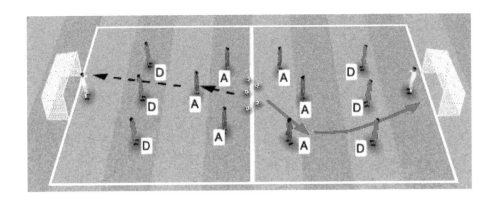

Progressions:

A GK starts with the ball and plays to the middle of the pitch to the attacking team.

Overload either team for different outcomes.

Have a time limit during which the attacking team must have an attempt on goal.

GK Learning Detail:

Technical: Technical response to the attempt on goal | Identify when and where to use top or bottom hand, and also when to use leg saves

Tactical: Positioning – observe the GK in relation to the ball but also the defending players | Ability to manoeuvre the ball out of the penalty area – wrist and hand strength

Psychological: Information/Communication to defenders – content, tone of voice, appropriateness of information | Ability to assess and execute their technical response with maximum speed

Physical: Footwork to cover the goal laterally | Diving and jumping actions from a standing stance | Set position and stance at point of contact | Don't be afraid to produce 'unorthodox' movement patterns away from traditional lines of thinking

Social/Environmental: Desire to defend the goal from *all* situations – even ones where there seems no hope in saving the ball

Outfield Learning Detail:

Technical: Defenders' ability to stay big and block shots (head and hips square onto the ball) | Pressure, balance, and the delaying of attackers | Attackers' shooting range and style of shot based upon the picture they see

Tactical: All outfield players' ability to adapt to the picture they see once the ball has been played in from a server | Speed and purpose of the attacking patterns

Psychological: Defenders' decisions on how, where, and when to press the ball and their timing to engage/win it | Do the attackers assess the defenders' and GK's positions early, to best inform how they approach the individual repetition

Physical: Defenders' abilities to decelerate and show away from goal | Can attackers adjust their bodies to receive and shoot in one movement | Overall balance and control of body when passing, moving, and striking on goal

Social/Environmental: Ruthlessness of the attackers to score, and of the defenders not to concede!

94

Goalkeeping Themes: Defending the goal against volleys and half volleys.

Practice Objectives: To challenge the GK to defend the goal against different types of volley from positions in and around the goal area. Attacking players will work on the timing of their contact and the technical/physical detail of volleying.

Description: The ball starts with player 1 who is around 12-15 yards away from goal. They play a ball to either server 1 or 2 at any height but allow them to lay off to player 2 who tries to score. If the GK parries the ball back towards the servers, they can have a rebound and if the GK secures the ball they can distribute the ball back to player 1 however they feel.

Progressions:

Change the distance and angle of player 1's starting point.

Have player 2 shooting from wider positions.

Build in a competition for all players involved.

GK Learning Detail:

Technical: Head position is crucial and will dictate the GK's stance and ability to keep their shape | Observe when to use leg saves | Look to repel and deflect the ball away rather than just letting the ball hit themselves | Which body part to use in order to be effective and not afraid to be 'unorthodox' | From volleys, pick up the flight and trajectory of the ball which will bring in top hand saves

Tactical: If the ball coming back from the server is bouncing – don't advance | Speed to adapt positioning based upon the travelling ball

Psychological: It's the GK vs the ball! | Desire to keep the ball out the net | To carry on giving 100% effort and focus in the face of adversity | Bravery to be hit on the body from a short-range distance | Speed of decision making in terms of how best to keep the ball out of the goal

Physical: Speed and co-ordination of body and limbs | Footwork patterns to re-adjust to the type of delivery from the wide server and to be in control of this movement pattern | Potentially backwards movements from volleys – observe this movement and emphasise dropping the shoulder rather than purely backpedalling

Social/Environmental: The practice is designed to really test the GKs in terms of how much success they will enjoy – make sure they understand that there will be goals and that any save from this range can be classified as success! | Have a competition to see who concedes the fewest goals if more than one GK is in the practice

Outfield Learning Detail:

The quality of the passing and setting of the ball from all players.

The timing of player 2's assessment and execution of the volley they've selected to use.

Control and balance during the execution of the technique.

The point of contact on the ball from player 2.

95

Goalkeeping Themes: Crossing scenarios with medium to long-range passing built in.

Practice Objectives: To allow the GK to practise longer-range passing and to work on opposed crossing situations. For the outfield players to work on defending and attacking different types of crosses from deep, and further towards the by-line.

Description: The ball will start from a wide position, as shown, and gets played into the GK who looks to the wide player on the right; they pass depending on their position and their pass must allow them to control the ball to drive towards. The wide player will then attack and cross the ball into a 3v3 scenario (the initial player who passed to the first GK will then join the attacking team). The attacking team will look to score in the first phase and the defenders will protect the goal. If the defending team secure or win the ball, they aim to play to the opposite GK or to the position from which the ball started. The pitch shown is 20x40 yards to encourage early crossing. If numbers allow, the initial player to start can stay in position and the third attacker starts in the main playing zone. After a pre-determined number of repetitions, the practice will switch ends – the same players can defend and attack or a rotation can occur.

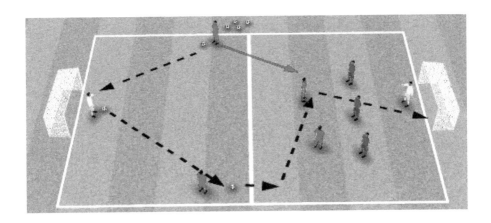

Progressions:

Adapt the pitch size and the numbers defending/attacking.

Overload/underload the attacking players to change the situation.

Use both left and right wings to attack.

GK Learning Detail:

Technical: First touch to play across the pitch | Quality and playability of the initial pass from the first GK | Head position is crucial and will dictate a GK's stance and ability to keep their shape | Observe when to use leg saves | Look to repel and deflect the ball away rather than letting the ball just hit themselves | Which body part to use in order to be effective and not afraid to be 'unorthodox' | From volleys or headers, pick up the flight and trajectory of the ball which will bring in top hand saves

Tactical: Positioning from the crossed ball – don't overcompensate at the front post | Assess whether left or right foot cross | Offer information to the defender to aid their defensive duties

Psychological: Assessment of the flight and trajectory of the cross – can they affect the ball | If not coming for the ball then look at the GK's recovery position and make sure they *don't* look to track the ball but turn their head to the anticipated point of contact from the attackers

Physical: Efficiency and control of movement laterally and vertically around the goal mouth | Speed of upper limbs and lower limbs | Observe the GK's head position upon their contact – is it close to the ball? Ability to generate power from a standing stance

Social/Environmental: The practice is designed to really test the GKs in terms of how much success they will enjoy – make sure they understand that there will be goals and that any save from this range can be classified as success! | Have a competition to see who concedes the fewest goals

Outfield Learning Detail:

Technical: The pass and cross detail from all attacking players | Technical proficiency of first time finishes with a focus on the attacking player's point of contact | Clearances from the defender – are they with the correct body part and are they with height and distance

Tactical: Defender(s)' protection of the goal and body shape/intention to do so |Attacking movement based upon the picture in front of them (defenders' positioning and the direction of the crosses) |Finishing type – is this appropriate based upon the position the attacker finds themselves in

Psychological: Concentration throughout the whole practice | Is the cross of appropriate detail for the attackers' positioning and the timing/movement of their runs?

Physical: Movement timing and adjustment in accordance with the ball | Attacking players' ability to create space away from the defender | Co-ordination and striking balance when crossing and finishing first time

Social/Environmental: Place emphasis on the attacking players playing at match tempo/intensity and being ruthless in front of goal – trying to score at every attempt – this applies to any rebounds off the GKs as well

96

Goalkeeping Themes: Defending the area and the goal in 1v1 scenarios.

Practice Objectives: To give the GK practice on dealing with a 1v1 situation in front of them. For the defender to work on their triggers and timing to press/engage the ball. For the attacking player to practice variations to beat a defender 1v1 and then beat the GK.

Description: The defender starts with the ball on the by-line and plays a long pass to the attacker. The attacker then advances towards the shaded grid (which they must enter before attacking the goal) to be met with the same defender who passed the ball. They then enter into a 1v1 duel. If the defender wins the ball, they become the attacker and can go towards the opposite goal in any way they want. In this practice, the same process as above can be taking place simultaneously on the other side of the pitch. If the GK secures the ball, they play back out to the starting point where the defenders and balls are located. The grid will vary depending on the age and ability of the players being worked with to bring in realistic distances.

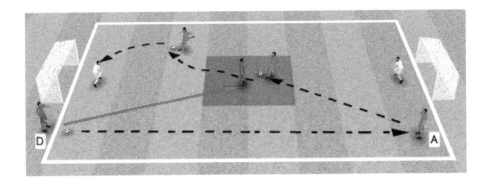

Progressions:

Potential to do a 2v2 practice or an overload practice.

Change the shaded grid size.

Take the middle grid out and play 'all in' with no restrictions.

Bring in a time limit for the attacker to shoot at goal.

GK Learning Detail:

Technical: Technical response based upon the finishing range (1v1, short or longer-range strike) | Ability to manoeuvre the ball away from immediate danger (hand shapes based upon the pace of the ball)

Tactical: Decision of when, where, and how to engage the ball and leave the goal area | Initial start position and adaptability in their positioning based upon how the picture changes

Psychological: Speed of assessment off the attacking player's first touch and their direction of movement | Don't guess or pre-empt too early what the attacking players will do – maintain a pro-active mindset to anticipate (there is a fine balance between anticipation and guesswork) | The decision whether to engage the ball will dictate coaching points – look at the defender's position when the GK engages; is it appropriate to get involved at that specific time

Physical: Ability to move with speed and control to defend the area initially from the combination play | Set position and balance upon the attacker's strike on goal | General speed and agility to change position quickly to respond to the movement of the ball | Ability to show an appropriate body position if engaging the ball for a 1v1 save

Social/Environmental: Build in some challenges, e.g. a point scoring system | Pair a GK up with one attacker to act as a team together – first to five goals for example | Focus on consistency of actions and appropriateness of decision making

Outfield Learning Detail:

If the GK is engaging the ball, observe the role of the defender – cover the goal.

Defender's speed and direction of pressure, and their ability to decelerate.

Defender's ability to use their body and limbs during physical contact.

Defender's relationship with the GK to work together to deny opportunities to shoot.

Attacker's ability to be unpredictable and open up spaces to shoot.

Attacker's desire to score and to assess the positioning and movements of the GK.

97

Goalkeeping Themes: Crossing and reaction saves – defending the goal to make big saves.

Practice Objectives: To provide the platform for GKs to be exposed to situations where the odds are against them; to keep the ball out of the goal they will need to make big 'match-defining' saves. For the attacking players, this exercise needs them to be clinical in front of goal. Defenders (if used) will work on last-ditch blocks, headers, and interceptions.

Description: The ball will start wide with player 1 or 2 who crosses the ball for an attacker to finish first time in either goal. This will be unopposed to begin with, and defenders or mannequins can be added as appropriate. If a larger group is working, then positions can be rotated.

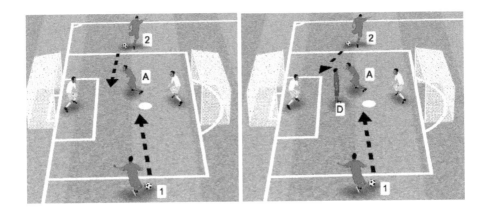

Progressions:

Change the crossers' positions (width and depth).

Add in more attackers or defenders.

Increase the distances between the goals to change the types of cross and the scenario in the middle.

GK Learning Detail:

Technical: Technical response that seeks to prevent rebounds on goal from either attacking player | How the GK keeps the ball out of the goal from player 2 – be adaptable and do not worry too much on 'how' to keep it out of the goal; observe head position with this detail

Tactical: Ability to cover the necessary space if the ball is squared to attacker 2, based upon their position and the pathway of the ball | GKs' positions in relation to the goal posts – don't overcompensate and come outside the line of the posts

Psychological: Assessment of attacker 1's first touch and how this impacts upon their decision of how and where to move | Allow the GK to try different techniques so they build up the confidence to develop their own style to defend the goal | Does the GK give up on possible lost causes? Or do they throw their body on the line

Physical: Key observation of each GK's set position following any strike on goal | When the GK is in motion, observe if the distance they need to cover requires arm movement – longer distances will need arms for travel | Work on the crossover step to cover more distance

Social/Environmental: Use the practice as a chance to develop a ruthless mentality to defend the goal!

Outfield Learning Detail:

Technical: Overall finishing and ball striking technique | Adaptability to assess the picture and respond technically in a consistent manner | Crossing quality and variety

Tactical: Observation of the GKs' positioning and how best to score based on the visual information available to them

Psychological: Early assessment of different types of finish to use | Attacker's ability to move into an early position to strike – depending on the flight and trajectory of the ball

Physical: Balance upon receiving touches and ball striking | Stability of striking technique and foot manipulation of the ball (side foot, laces, curling, etc.)

Social/Environmental: Being clinical in front of goal and enjoying scoring – also from any rebounds from the GK | Make sure the attackers finish the repetition with a goal when possible

98

Goalkeeping Themes: Maintaining possession under pressure and in tight areas.

Practice Objectives: To give the GKs an environment where they are a central part of a possession practice. It allows them to work on their quality and consistency of first touch, ability to play under pressure, and proficiency to pick different passes. For the outfield players, this is a chance to work on different passing patterns and combinations and to use the GKs as much as possible.

Description: The possession practice is in a grid of varying distance – the example shown is 25x40 yards. There are two teams that aim to make a certain number of passes whilst using the GKs as often as possible (as suitable). The ball will always start from a GK if the ball leaves the grid or the number of passes required has been achieved. Different constraints can be put on the outfield players at the coach's discretion.

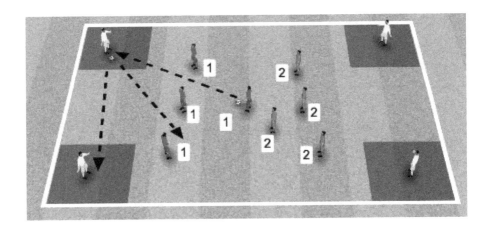

Progressions:

Adapt the grid size and constraints to change the focus of the session – a tighter grid will lead to less reaction time and more pressure.

Keep the GKs in a grid where they can't be tackled to build confidence and to recognise the picture in front of them – good for younger or novice GKs.

Put the GKs on a touch limit to encourage quick play, enabling the ball to be recycled quickly.

GK Learning Detail:

Technical: First touch detail – this should be dictated by the direction that GKs want to play | Quality of the pace and purpose of their passing | Being comfortable using both feet at all times

Tactical: Have a plan before the ball is received | Identify when to play to feet or space | Developing a variety of passing skills

Psychological: Control and composure when in possession of the ball | Clear thinking to analyse the best pass and option at that specific time | Read the play and be in a pro-active position to play | Support away from pressure to give themselves more time to play the ball

Physical: General co-ordination and balance before, and during, receipt of the ball | The amount of power the GK can generate and its appropriateness to the pass they are playing | Ability to manipulate the ball when in possession and put fade/spin on the ball

Social/Environmental: Focus on the tempo which the GK is playing

Outfield Learning Detail:

Individual movement and body shape to receive the ball.

Willingness to get on the ball and to trust the GK to use them in open play.

Potential rotation of players to create space to play.

Don't delay if a player is going to play to the GK; the more time taken, the more pressure they're likely to be under.

99

Goalkeeping Themes: Maintaining possession and building attacks – using the whole width of the playing area to bring in different support positions.

Practice Objectives: To give the GKs an environment where they are a central part of a possession practice. It allows them to work on their quality and consistency of first touch, ability to play under pressure, and proficiency to pick different passes. For the outfield players, this is a chance to work on different passing patterns and combinations and to use the GKs as much as possible.

Description: The possession practice is in a grid of varying distance – the example shown is 25x40 yards. The GK has the whole width of the grid to operate in (unopposed or opposed). There are two teams that aim to work the ball from their GK to the opposite GK. The practice will continue and the team that gave the ball to the GK will look to then attack the other way. If the ball is turned over, the team that wins the ball can look to attack either GK to begin with. The ball will always start from a GK if it leaves the grid or the number of passes required has been achieved. Different constraints can be put on the outfield players at the coach's discretion.

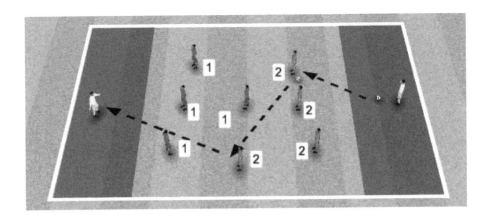

Progressions:

Bring in some wide players (outside the playing grid) for the GKs to look to find with their distribution.

Allow the GK to restart the practice using any kind of distribution.

GK Learning Detail:

Technical: First touch detail – this should be dictated by the direction they want to play | Quality of the pace and purpose of passing | Being comfortable using both feet at all times

Tactical: Have a plan before the ball is received | Identify when to play to feet or space | Developing a variety of passing skills

Psychological: Control and composure when in possession of the ball | Clear thinking to analyse the best pass and option at that specific time | Read the play and be in a pro-active position to play | Support away from pressure to give themselves more time to play the ball

Physical: General co-ordination and balance before and during receipt of the ball | The amount of power the GK can generate and its appropriateness to the pass they are playing | Ability to manipulate the ball when in possession and put fade/spin upon the ball

Social/Environmental: Focus on the tempo which the GK is playing

Outfield Learning Detail:

Individual movement and body shape to receive the ball.

Willingness to get on the ball and to trust the GK to use them in open play.

Potential rotation of players to create space to play.

Don't delay if a player is going to play to the GK; the more time taken, the more pressure they're likely to be under.

Encourage dribbling as well as passing possession.

100

Goalkeeping Themes: General shot stopping and the prevention of goal scoring opportunities.

Practice Objectives: To give the GKs lots of 1v2 scenarios – looking at triggers for engaging the ball and how to communicate with defenders. For the defenders, this exercise works on where and when to press, alongside efforts to delay the attackers. Attackers will work on quick combination play, exploiting and opening up spaces, and being clinical in front of goal.

Description: There are two versions of this setup happening at the same time. Pitch 1 is the first phase where the attacking team starts with the ball and attacks the goal. The second pitch is the second phase; if the GK secures the ball, they look to play through the target zone at the top of the pitch. The size of the pitch is 20x30 yards and this should vary depending on the age/ability of players. If the defender wins the ball, they can play to the GK to pass through the same target zone, or they can run with the ball off the pitch – exploiting the space to do so.

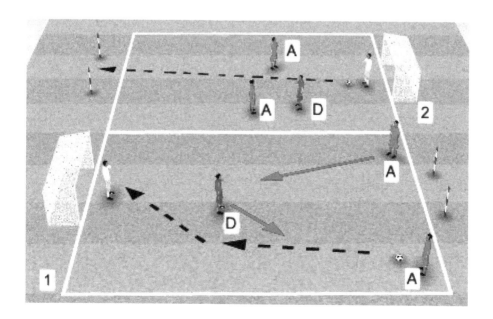

Progressions:

Have a time limit for the attacking team to get a shot on goal.

Rotate players regularly so they can go up against different opponents.

The GK starts with the ball and passes out to the attacking players.

Alternate which attacking player initiates the attack on goal.

GK Learning Detail:

Technical: Technical response based upon the finishing range (1v1, short or longer-range strike) | Ability to manoeuvre the ball away from immediate danger (hand shapes based upon the pace of the ball) | If the ball is squared to the second attacker, can the GK cover the ground to make blocks and last-ditch efforts to keep the ball out

Tactical: Make the ball the priority | Decision of when, where, and how to engage the ball and leave the goal area | Initial start position and adaptive positioning based upon how the picture changes

Psychological: Speed of assessment off the attacking players' first touches and their direction of movement | Don't guess or pre-empt too early what the attacking players will do; maintain a pro-active mindset to anticipate – there's a fine balance between anticipation and guesswork | The decision whether to engage the ball will dictate coaching points – look at the defenders' positions when the GK engages; is it appropriate to get involved at that specific time

Physical: Ability to move with speed and control to defend the area, initially, from the combination play | Set position and balance upon the attacker's strike on goal | General speed and agility to change position quickly, to respond to the movement of the ball | Ability to show an appropriate body position if engaging the ball for a 1v1 save

Social/Environmental: Build in some challenges, e.g. point scoring system | Focus on the consistency of actions and the appropriateness of decision making

Outfield Learning Detail:

If the GK is engaging the ball, observe the role of the defender – cover the goal.

Defender's speed and direction of pressure, and their ability to decelerate.

Defender's ability to use their body and limbs during physical contact.

Defender's relationship with the GK to work together to deny opportunities to shoot.

Attackers' ability to be unpredictable and open up spaces to shoot.

Attackers' desire to score and to assess the positioning and movement of the GK.

Both attackers' ability to move the defender to create space.

101

Goalkeeping Themes: Balls played across the box – when to engage/when to defend the goal.

Practice Objectives: To allow the GK to work on judging balls played across the box at different heights and trajectories with a focus on the 6-12-yard range (second 6-yard box). For the attackers to work on finishing from different positions and with different parts of their body. Defenders, if used, have the opportunity to work on clearances and dealing with different runs from the attacking players.

Description: The attacker in the wide position volleys the ball (left or right foot) across the box in varying ways to create different flights, bounces, and ball speeds for an attacker to try to score. Picture 2 shows two attackers with one defender but the defender can be optional to give the players more situations where the defence has been taken out of the game.

Progressions:

Change the depth and width of the crossing player.

Work with the attacking players to start in different positions to give the GK new challenges in terms of shot contact points.

GK Learning Detail:

Technical: Technical response that seeks to prevent rebounds on goal from either attacking player | How the GK keeps the ball out of the goal from player 2 – be adaptable and do not worry too much on 'how' to keep the ball out of the goal – observe head position with this detail | If engaging the ball in the space, think about hand shape and arm extension – the pace on the ball will (in part) dictate this but make sure the GK looks to get maximum distance and contact on the ball if they can't secure it

Tactical: Left or right footed cross and how that affects the GK's start position | Re-positioning to defend the goal based upon the point of contact from an attacking player

Psychological: Bravery from the GK to attack and defend the space in front of them | Assessment of the ball – whether a volley or half volley, ball flights will be very random | Allow the GK to try different techniques so they build up the confidence to develop their own style to defend the goal | Does the GK give up on possible lost causes? Or do they throw their body on the line

Physical: Key observation on the GK's set position upon a strike on goal | When the GK is in motion, observe if the distance they need to cover requires arm movement – longer distances will need arms for travel | Work on the crossover step to cover more distance

Social/Environmental: Use the practice as a chance to develop a ruthless mentality to defend the goal!

Outfield Learning Detail:

Variation from the crossing player – encourage different ball contacts to throw up different challenges for all players.

Types of finishes the attacker(s) are able to produce – are they appropriate to the pace, direction, and trajectory of the ball.

The timing and assessment of the attacker(s)' runs and movement onto the ball.

The defending player's ability to read the danger/main threats and clear the ball.

Conviction and purpose in all actions from the outfield players.

Other Coaching Books from Bennion Kearny

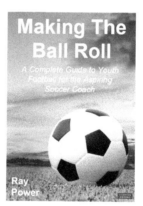

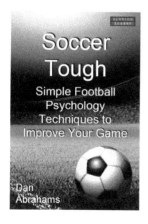

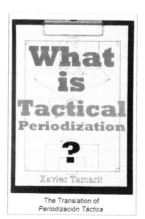

Deliberate Soccer Practice

50 Defending Football Exercises to Improve Decision-Making

Ray Power

Andy Elleray

65 Goalkeeper Training Exercises

Modern Games-Based Soccer Drills for Shot Stopping, Footwork, Distribution, and More

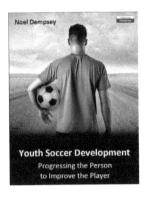

Noel Dempsey

Youth Soccer Development

Progressing the Person to Improve the Player

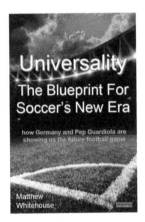

Universality

The Blueprint For Soccer's New Era

how Germany and Pep Guardiola are showing us the future football game

Matthew Whitehouse

BUILDING A SUCCESSFUL HIGH SCHOOL SPORTS PROGRAM

DeAngelo Wiser

★★★★★
Paul Webb Academy

Strength Training for Goalkeepers

Soccer Tough II

Advanced Psychology Techniques for Footballers

Dan Abrahams

SOCCER TRAINING BLUEPRINTS

15 Ready-to-Run Sessions for Outstanding Attacking Play

James Jordan

THE FOOTBALLER'S JOURNEY:
REAL-WORLD ADVICE ON BECOMING AND REMAINING A PROFESSIONAL FOOTBALLER

DEAN CASLAKE & GUY BRANSTON

Lightning Source UK Ltd.
Milton Keynes UK
UKHW050229310719

347095UK00009B/97/P